BABY BUMPS

BABY BUMPS

FROM PARTY GIRL TO PROUD MAMA,
AND ALL THE MESSY MILESTONES ALONG THE WAY

by

Nicole "Snooki" Polizzi

RUNNING PRESS
PHILADELPHIA · LONDON

© 2013 by Nicole Polizzi
Published by Running Press,
A Member of the Perseus Books Group

Books published by Running Press are available at special discounts for bulk
purchases in the United States by corporations, institutions, and other
organizations. For more information, please contact the Special Markets
Department at the Perseus Books Group, 2300 Chestnut Street, Suite 200,
Philadelphia, PA 19103, or call (800) 810-4145, ext. 5000, or
e-mail special.markets@perseusbooks.com.

ISBN 978-0-7624-5162-3
Library of Congress Control Number: 2013950312

E-book ISBN 978-0-7624-5165-4

9   8   7   6   5   4   3   2
Digit on the right indicates the number of this printing

Cover design by Dan Cantada
Interior Design by Maria Taffera Lewis
Edited by Jennifer Kasius
Typography: Gotham, Chronicle, and Thirsty Rough

Running Press Book Publishers
2300 Chestnut Street
Philadelphia, PA 19103-4371

Visit us on the web!
www.runningpress.com

Dedication

This book is dedicated to my beautiful son, Lorenzo.
Without him, I wouldn't know the true meaning of life and
how awesome it feels to be a MILF!

I'd also like to dedicate this book to my fiancé, Jionni.
Without him, I wouldn't have Lorenzo
or unforgettable gas pains when pregnant.

CONTENTS

Introduction

My pregnancy began with the thought, "Holy shit! My egg hatched!" I didn't think I could conceive. Over a lot of years of not using birth control (I know, bad idea), nothing ever happened. I was shocked my body actually did what it was supposed to do. But after the amazement, I got a rebound reality check and thought, *What am I going to do? Can I really pull this off?*

When Jionni and I realized we were knocked up, we weren't engaged. We'd been together for a year and had had plenty of ups and downs. We'd only just settled into a great, stable relationship. I thought our bumps were behind us. But as it turned out, a big one, the biggest, was starting to develop.

There was no question. We were in love; we wanted to keep the baby. But that didn't mean I felt ready to be a mom. I was 24. Jionni and I both still lived with our parents. I had next to no experience dealing with kids, and zero exposure to infants. Babysitting jobs in high school? Uh, no. (Hey, I don't blame my neighbors. I wouldn't have hired myself!) I'd never held a baby or changed a diaper. Wait, that's not entirely true. I did try to change a diaper once, but I had to stop mid-wipe and run out the room. I just didn't *like* kids.

I still wanted to have some, though. I figured I'd grow to like kids when I was older myself, like 27 or 28. Then I'd see about becoming a young, sexy mom with four tan babies. So my plans were fast forwarded. Of course I was nervous! The idea of being responsible for a small helpless creature—other than myself—had me quaking in my booties.

In my fantasies about becoming a mom, I blipped over the pregnancy part. Good call. Those nine months turned me into a slobbering bitch from HELL. I wanted to crawl in a hole. The "kill me now" queasiness was one among dozens of miseries, all of which I'm going to describe in florid, fetid detail in this book. Better brace yourself for some serious disgustingness. You might have to read with one hand over your eyes and the other holding your nose. Pregnancy is not for the faint of heart *or* bowels. It's a leaky, oozing, gassy mess. If anyone tells you different, she's sugar coating like a candy factory.

According to my doctor, my conception and pregnancy were "easy." We didn't need test tubes or turkey basters. No frozen eggs defrosted in a microwave. No scary bleeding, false labor, or mandatory bed rest. We didn't have to race to the hospital in the middle of the night. I wasn't wheeled on a gurney into emergency surgery, screaming, "Save my baby! I don't care if I live or die, but SAVE MY BABY!" For once in my life, I got through a summer with minimal drama. Calling a pregnancy "easy" is a relative term, though. Mine didn't seem easy to me, not by a long shot! I couldn't wait for it to end.

And then, it did. Lorenzo was born in late August. Pregnancy was over, but motherhood was just getting started. Despite my nerves and fears, being a mom came naturally. Moments after the birth, when the nurse plopped Lorenzo on my chest, I knew instinctually how to hold him and talk to him. And if I hadn't, I would have had to figure it out ASAP. Motherhood comes at you like a speeding Range Rover. You have to throw away doubt and immediately care for your child. You might want to take a two-week vacation after pregnancy and labor. But your baby needs you *now*. You hit the shit running. That's actually a good thing. You don't have any time to worry about whether you're a good mom. In fact, if you do have lots of time to think about it, then you're not doing it right.

As I write this, I've been a mom for nine months, as long as I was pregnant. I'm not scared anymore. The opposite. I'm strong and confident. Motherhood reminds me of this line from *A Midsummer Night's Dream*: "And though she be but little, she is fierce." (Yeah, I can quote Shakespeare.) Until I had a baby, I had no idea what it meant to be fierce. I thought I did, but I was way off. I went from wearing leopard print to really feeling like a leopard. Just try to touch my baby, and the claws will come out.

Not to say motherhood is easy. It's natural, but it's a challenge. Jionni and I live in a constant shit storm. I do mean that literally. The shit actually rains down on us sometimes. And guess what? I don't care. I clean crap off the walls, and I laugh because Lorenzo is the most precious, incredible thing in my life. I got through the pregnancy, the labor and delivery, and that so-called fourth trimester when Lorenzo was a newborn. I feel happier and stronger than ever. If I can do it and come out in one piece, anyone can.

My so-called ordinary road to motherhood was anything but. It was an *extraordinary* roller coaster ride. Every day of the experience blew my mind—and blew up my body to unbelievable proportions. No matter how uneventful a pregnancy might seem to outside observers, to the woman who's experiencing it, it's enormous and epic and makes her feel like she's the first woman who's ever done it. I know that people have been getting pregnant since the dawn of time, that billions of women have done it before me, and billions more will do it after I'm long gone. But when you feel life growing inside you, the most basic, common aspect of human existence seems like a friggin' miracle.

One tiny baby can change the world. Lorenzo has certainly changed mine. Since my "egg hatched!" moment, my life has changed 180 degrees—all for the better. I'm a different person now. I love who I've become. Like too-trendy clothes from another time, parts of my old personality don't look right on me anymore. I'm sure people who think of me as a wasted smurf on *Jersey Shore* might find it hard to believe that, these days, the only bottles I care about are full of formula or milk. I'd rather go to the gym than a club. The only men who see my boobs are my fiancé and my son. Instead of sleeping all morning, I'm up early playing with Lorenzo. While he sleeps, I just stare at him. Don't get me wrong. I am and will always be true to myself. I still want to look good and have fun. But my definition of "fun" has been turned inside out.

This book is about what I went through, my ordinary/ extraordinary journey from Party Girl to Proud Mama. Since I'm not a doctor or a childbirth expert, I'm not about to rattle off advice on that level. I wouldn't want to. I am the last person to tell others how to live and what decisions to make. I don't judge, and I don't preach. That is not my style at all. I *am* an expert on myself, though, and I'm just bursting to tell you my whole story, from the first pee stick to the last breast pump. Warning: You will not find "I'm a radiant pregnant woman, watch me glow!" stories in here. That's not how it was for me. I want to tell the not-so-glamorized truth about the dirty job of becoming a mom. Maybe other women really do have the smiling, rocking chair pregnancy that you see on the cover of other books about it. I know each pregnancy story is unique. But we all deal with a lot of the same issues and weirdness. I hope sharing my crazy thoughts and gross moments will give readers some relief when they have theirs.

Basically, I feel your gas pain.

After reading this book, you'll definitely feel mine!

Chapter 1

Three Out of Six Pee Sticks Can't Be Wrong

—ഗ—

Before I write another word, I have to say the truth. Pregnancy is disgusting, and I hated it. It hurts to breathe. You pee yourself. You become obsessed with farting and pooping.

It takes about five minutes to figure that out for a lot of pregnant women. As soon as they put their heads in a toilet to puke that first morning, they realize, "Creating human life is a nightmare!" Yes, it's beautiful and a miracle, whatever. But it's no picnic. It's like a horror movie, with blood and farts and fluids flying everywhere, then later, boobs and milk spurting out of control. I am not shitting you. When I was pregnant, I could barely shit myself from constipation.

Before I even knew I was pregnant, I was having a great time with my hot husband (I called him my husband even though we were just boyfriend-girlfriend then). When we started out, we were a one-night stand on the Jersey Shore. He was just some beefy guido I kidnapped from Karma to get busy with. We had a good time, but in the morning, I thought, *I'll never see this guy again.* Before leaving the shore that summer, though, I ripped his number out of the house phone book. I thought he was forgettable—I could barely remember his name—but then I found myself thinking about him and wanting to see him again. When filming ended, I decided to text him. I still didn't think it would be a major relationship. He was hot and might be a friend with benefits. We started hanging out a lot. Before long, I realized, *Not just a smush buddy. It's more than that.* A little while after that, I realized, *Not just a boyfriend. He's the sauce to my meatball.* I simply couldn't do better. Jionni was tan, sexy, good in the sack, and hysterical. What more could a girl want? Plus, there was the intangible factor: I just loved him. I missed him when we were apart for a day. I *craved* him. I could not imagine life without him. He felt the same way about me. I'd been through years of soul searching for my dream boy. I thought it was the hardest thing in the world to find a good man and fall in love. Turned out to be incredibly easy. A one-night stand turned into the love of my life.

A year later, we were pregnant. Maybe it shouldn't have been such a surprise. Breaking news: If you don't use birth control, you might get knocked up. We did use condoms in the beginning, when he was a random guy I picked up at a club in Seaside three summers ago. But as soon as Jionni and I fell in love and decided to be exclusive, we stopped. No discussion. No, "Hey, we'd better be super careful." We smushed like drunk bunnies without bothering with protection. Of course, it was crazy pants. It was like a sexual high wire act or a game of Russian roulette using Jionni's sperm for bullets.

It might be possible I subconsciously wanted to get knocked up by him—or to see if I could. I'd never been pregnant before. I thought I was infertile. We had a lot of unprotected sex. Like, a lot. But every month, my period came. It was late sometimes from traveling and going wild. But it always showed up eventually. I would feel relieved and disappointed at the same time.

Then, in December 2011, my period was a week late. It'd never been *that* late before. I thought to myself, *Hey, hon, get a pregnancy test!* But I blew it off. It was the holidays. We were traveling a lot. I forgot about my lateness for another couple of weeks. We celebrated the New Year in Las Vegas and partied hard. A few days later, we flew to Los Angeles. When I was packing, I thought, "Should pack some tampons." And then I tried to think back to my last period. When had that been? November? I couldn't remember.

We were sitting in our hotel, and I said, "I'm really late. Beyond unfashionably late. I might've skipped a whole period. Does that happen?" It'd never happened to me before.

Jionni went out and bought a pregnancy test. We went into the bathroom together. Jionni sat on the edge of the tub while I whizzed. Then we hunched over the stick, staring nervously and waiting for something to happen. The window turned pink.

"Holy shit!" we said, and started giggling.

Then, at the same time, we said, "We're keeping it."

I glanced in the bathroom mirror, rubbed my tummy and grinned. I pictured a little spermie and eggie chilling together in there. A baby. Really? Me as a mom?

Yup. We weren't exactly ready for the challenge of parenthood. We weren't married or engaged. So what? We were in love, and made a baby in love.

Look, we weren't delusional about the situation. It wasn't the ideal time or stage of life to get knocked up. But as soon as we realized what was happening, we shifted focus. Our lives changed on a dime. Fingers snap—*poof!*—we made the change. It really was that fast. But it wasn't easy!

Before we got *really* excited, though, we thought it'd be a good idea to confirm the first test's results. Jionni ran out and got five more pregnancy tests.

He was back in the room within a half an hour. He unwrapped five sticks and had them lined up and ready to go. I doused them all, one after the other. I could have hosed down a dozen. I never have a hard time peeing. I am a whizzing champion.

The results this time were mixed. Three said negative, and two were positive. According to our six sticks, I was half pregnant—which I knew wasn't possible.

So was I knocked up or not?

We called the helpline number on the instruction sheet and talked to a lady who explained that, basically, you can get a false negative, but if any test shows a positive, you are way pregnant. We then called Jionni's pregnant sister who said the same thing. But those three negatives bugged me. I wasn't 1,000 percent convinced that the three positives were right. If there was any chance I wasn't preggers, we wanted to change that. Once the idea of having a baby took hold, we couldn't wait to do it. It wasn't on the radar an hour before, but now it *had* to happen, right away. We said, "Let's do it!"

Jionni and I were so excited at the thought of becoming parents, we wanted to guarantee it. So right away, we ripped off our clothes and hopped in the sack. It was a total smush fest of laughing and saying, "Woohoo, we're making a baby! I'M GONNA BE A MOM!" not knowing for sure we already had a little baby on board. That was a fun and crazy night. We didn't go to sleep until dawn. We flew back to Jersey a day later and went straight to the doctor. He confirmed the great news. A little zygote was definitely doing handsprings in my uterus, and had been getting cozy in there for two months already. We were officially pregnant. Yes! It was the perfect way to kick off 2012.

What an incredible feeling! I'd just been living my life, but my body had been up to something amazing while I wasn't paying attention. The fact that Jionni and I reacted the same way to the pregnancy proved to me beyond a doubt that we were meant to be together. It was only a matter of time before we got engaged.

Bonus: Just as I'd always dreamed, my future husband's name ended with a vowel.

Here's Jionni

Nicole and I hadn't been using birth control for a while, but I didn't think about whether she would get pregnant any more than she did. I was one of those people who thought, *It won't happen to me.* And then it did.

My first thought? *Oh shit, oh shit, oh shit!* Not in a terrified way. Well, a little shocked. I was just as excited as Nicole. I knew we'd be together forever, and I always wanted to marry her. The surprise pregnancy just meant we'd do it sooner than expected. Neither one of us had any hesitation. No regrets, no doubts. Not once did we think, *Should we do this?* It was "yes" from the first pee stick, all the way through. My two brothers and sister have kids, and they're all happy with their families. I thought, *It's my turn now. I'm going to have a family.*

My first pregnancy chore: cleaning out the junk. I threw away the cigarettes and vodka bottles, and mentally closed the trash can lid on all of that for the next seven months. I know a lot of people recall *Jersey Shore* and think I'm a hopeless drunk. Not true. One day, I was a drinker and a sometimes smoker. The next? Completely sober and cigarette-free. It wasn't so hard. I just made up my mind to cut it out, and that was that. I might've wanted a drink in an abstract way, like, "I'm starving, get me a scotch." Smoking and drinking had always been fun stuff I enjoyed doing, but it wasn't something I needed. I didn't crave alcohol or nicotine like an addict. I peed on those sticks, and flushed away the desire to drink and smoke. I never wavered about that. No fetus of mine was going to swim around in a uterus full of vodka, batting away floating cigarette butts and olives.

Soon after our discovery, I went to a club. The waitress kept pushing cocktails on me. I kept turning her down. She seemed confused. Usually, when I go to a club, I party my ass off. That was my reputation. I realized I was in a bind. If I wasn't hammering cocktails, people would wonder why. They might come up with theories. Whenever you see a friend switch off alcohol with a sneaky smile on her face, the wheels start turning. You don't need to be a nuclear physicist to figure that one out. I asked the waitress for a seltzer and cranberry juice, figuring that would pass for a real drink.

"You sure you don't want vodka in that?" she asked.

"I'm sure," I said. She gave me a strange look.

I hate secrets. Usually, I can't keep my mouth shut. I was dying to share our news. But I had to tell my parents first. I was scared to tell them, especially my dad. My career meant a lot to him. He ran the business. BTW, my career isn't just falling on my ass, or sitting on it, for a reality TV show. I create products for my brand—lipstick, perfume, sunglasses, etc. I also write books (you're holding one right now) and do promotional appearances. A pregnancy threw a giant squirrel monkey wrench into it all, but mainly the TV part. Would fans of *Jersey Shore* want to watch me fat and sober?

Doubtful.

If my reality TV run ended because of the pregnancy, I'd be fine with it. I'd walk away in a second if I had to choose between fame and family. Dad put family first, too, of course. He always had, and always would. I worried that he'd say the timing was wrong, and that I shouldn't have a baby until my career had fallen off.

I didn't want to hear it, so I avoided my parents. I didn't call them for a week, which was an eternity for us. I usually talk to Mom and Dad a few times a day. When I finally called, I said, "I have something to tell you."

Dad said, "We already know."

The week of black ops silence made them suspicious. Mom heard I'd been to the doctor. They knew that if I had any bad health news, I would have called them while still in the paper gown on the examining room table. If I had good news and didn't call, they figured it had to be a pregnancy.

"But you've got your whole life ahead of you," said Dad. He meant my life as a celebrity. He knew, as I did, that my so-called fame had a time limit. Opportunities flowed my way *now*, but they'd stop someday. I'd been smart about saving so far. Would it be enough to raise a child? Jionni always said that if my career ended, he'd step up and support us. He already had a couple of businesses—selling t-shirts and an ATM company—that were doing well. Plus, I didn't need to live large. That was not my style, never had been. When I wasn't traveling or shooting a show, I slept in my childhood bedroom at home.

I did get a little pissed off at Dad. He talked to me like I was 15. But I wasn't a pregnant high school dropout. I was 24, had a career, had savings, and was in a serious relationship with a man who loved me. I'd always dreamed that one day I'd be a MILF with adorable tan babies. The surprise pregnancy just moved the dream up a couple of years.

"Dad, it's okay. I can make my own decisions. This is what I want," I told him.

Parents can't help but feel anxious about their children. Dad was just worried about me and how I'd support my baby. His brain naturally flowed in that direction. The guy carted around a plastic box full of my contracts and important business papers. He just didn't want me to struggle. To him, not struggling meant keeping my career going as long as possible to save money for later.

Mom was upset, too. She was thinking about another piece of paper: a marriage license. It was a generational thing. Of course, I wanted to get married to Jionni. We were committed and didn't need to rush to the altar before the baby was born just for the sake of . . . what exactly? Our baby wouldn't be loved harder because we were married. Our relationship was as secure as Fort Knox. Plus, I didn't want to be huge and nauseous—and sober—at my own wedding! No way! My vision of our wedding had me in an amazing dress, with an open bar and a hot DJ (paging Pauly D). It'd be a raucous party, and I'd look smoking hot in all the photos. The wedding would have to wait until after the baby was born.

My parents never tried to talk me out of it. But they did question whether I was ready to be responsible for another human life. I hadn't always been the most mature, upstanding citizen, as everyone knows. But I'd grown up a lot. In the last year, I'd more or less stopped getting wasted. I was in great physical shape. I'd been working hard and doing things I never thought I'd do, like designing flip-flops and writing novels. It'd be a stretch to say I'd magically transformed into the most mature and responsible woman on earth. But I wasn't the same 21-year-old drunk girl who was dragged off the beach in handcuffs by the cops. Everyone knows someone who turned her life around when she had a baby. I felt like my life had already made a hard turn in the right direction. The baby would only seal the deal.

My parents and I didn't talk for a few days after that first phone call. I didn't want to hear any negativity. But they came around to the positive very quickly. Within a week, Mom and Dad accepted the pregnancy and started to get excited about being grandparents. Jionni's parents were already grandparents five times over. They were thrilled to have another bambino on the way.

Next up, Jionni and I would tell our closest friends. We decided to hold off on that until we were sure the baby was healthy. The major prenatal testing to check for abnormalities happens at the twelve-week mark. Since I was already eight weeks along, we had to keep the secret for another month. That was going to be hard. We were dying to spread the news.

Despite being in my life for a while already, Jionni still wasn't used to living in a fish bowl. He didn't realize that a pregnancy had to be treated like a state secret. One slip of the tongue and it was out of our control. He told, like, twenty people. One of them must have told a friend, who told a friend. Suddenly, the story got leaked to the media. They were all over it the next day.

You'd think I'd committed a terrorist act by the way the press reacted. The "Is-she-or-isn't-she?" headlines were insane. The shock and horror were ridiculous. Blogs and gossip rags came down on me hard, as if I were the first pregnant 24-year-old single woman in history. It sucked! I tried to stem the rumors by denying the pregnancy. I'm not really superstitious, but it felt wrong to say I wasn't having a baby when I was. I worried that I was cursing the pregnancy.

I started to feel guilty, too. My friends heard about it from another source. I quickly sent an email to my core group that said, "No false alarm. It's real." Most of them were happy for us, but we also caught some doubt from a few with the "Are you *sure*?" questions. I know they were just being protective and were concerned about how the media would react. (Badly, just as they feared.)

The heat came at us from every direction. We had to lie outright to some people. I hated keeping the truth from anyone, including my fans. Besides, I wanted to scream it from the rooftops, not bite my tongue. But it just wasn't the right time. Imagine telling the world, "We're having a baby!" and then something went wrong and I had a miscarriage. We'd have to say, "Er, never mind." I wouldn't want my misery played out on magazine covers.

The absolute worst was denying the pregnancy to talk show hosts on TV while promoting *Jersey Shore*. The rumor mill was grinding away like cage dancers at a strip club. Kelly Ripa and others tried to get me to admit the truth on their show. Andy Cohen grilled me to a crisp about it on *Watch What Happens: Live*. The next time I went on his show, he made me swear on a Bible I wouldn't lie to him again. On another show, the host served Jenni Farley (aka JWOWW) and me glasses of beer. I raised the glass and let the beer touch my lips. Just a touch. I didn't drink a drop of it. But when I put the glass to my mouth, the host went nuts, saying, "You're not pregnant. The beer was a test!" As soon as the segment was over, I went backstage and cried. I was terrified that letting the beer touch my lips would hurt the baby. How fucked up was that of the host? She knew I didn't want to talk about the pregnancy rumors, so she put me on the spot and tried to force me to drink alcohol? It was beyond rude and possibly dangerous. All so she could bust me? I'll never do her show again.

Valentine's Day rolled around. I've had a few disappointing February 14ths in my life. Ugh, not fun. It's much better when my man goes all out. Rose petals on the bed, Champagne, a stuffed teddy bear holding a heart, a singing card. I love it all. Nothing is too cheesy. On Valentine's Day, 2012, I was twelve weeks pregnant and beyond stressed from keeping the news under lock and key.

Here's Jionni

Even though we agreed to postpone a wedding until after the baby, I thought it was important to propose as soon as possible. I wanted Nicole to know I would be at her side. She should feel secure that I was committed. I didn't want to get married just because of the baby. But the baby did make me want to propose. Nicole was so emotionally crazy, I hoped being engaged would give her comfort.

The plan was to surprise her. I managed to buy the ring and make a reservation at the W Hotel in Hoboken for Valentine's Day night without her knowing. Our room had a balcony that looked over the Hudson River. I did it up right. Flowers on the floor. Chocolate-dipped strawberries. Champagne. But she wasn't into it. The flower smell gave her a headache, and she wouldn't drink the Champagne, not even a sip. I wanted her to come out on the balcony with me to look at the view while I gave her my gift. But it was freezing, and she refused come outside. We argued on either side of the balcony door for a few minutes. I started to get really cold, so I just handed her the gift and said, "I got you something. It doesn't fit me. I hope it fits you."

She unwrapped the box. Inside was the ring. I didn't think she'd turn me down, but I was nervous she might not like the style of the ring. I was bracing for her to start crying again. She'd been like an open faucet for weeks.

She put on the ring. Her chin and lip started quivering and twitching. She burst out crying in such a dramatic way, I didn't think it was for real. I'm still standing in the freezing balcony, and she's inside the room, blubbering.

"So . . . yes?" I asked.

She screamed, "Yes!"

I came in from the cold and wrapped her up in my arms.

The ring was awesome. A five-carat princess cut diamond. Jionni designed it with the jeweler based on comments I'd made. Throughout the pregnancy, whenever I got upset or annoyed—like a thousand times a day—I looked at the sparkler on my finger and I felt better. It was a stunner! You couldn't not stare at it, which actually caused a problem. If we came out with the engagement news, then it'd be obvious we were pregnant. So we had *another* thing we wanted to tell the world, but had to keep quiet. I wore the ring, but turned it around so the stone wasn't so obvious.

After thirteen weeks along, we did the tests and learned that the fetus was healthy and the pregnancy was stable. We made our happy announcements with the help of *Us Weekly*. It was such a relief! I could go shopping for baby stuff and bigger clothes without having to lie or hide.

Instantly, the jokes started, like how my baby would be the spawn of Satan, or that he'd walk right out of my over-stretched vagina. People I'd never met were saying I would be a tragic mom, that social services should be called, that my baby would have Fetal Alcohol Syndrome, and worse.

I didn't like it. Who would? But I tried not to get offended. That was just the press doing their job—which was to trash my unborn baby. I'd been hearing the takedowns for four years already—decline of Western Civilization, Mayan Apocalypse, blah, blah, and blah. Some public figures totally freaked out when haters bashed them on social and traditional media. I just couldn't get that upset. Maybe my layers of spray tan created a shield against the negativity. It just didn't make sense to take it personally. The mean Tweeters didn't know me personally, so how could I take it that way? As long as I knew I was going to be a great mom, everyone else could suck it.

Chapter 2

The Endless Hangover

After we got engaged, Jionni and I talked about moving into a fantasy house that was custom made for us. We'd have a gym, a movie room, six bedrooms, a pool, a man cave, a walk-in closet for me, the works. I made some calls and found out that building our dream house from the bottom up would take at least a year, if not longer. In the meantime, we decided to move into the basement at Jionni's parents' house in northern New Jersey and stay there for the length of the pregnancy and for a while after the birth. His family was into it. Jionni's two brothers and sister lived within a mile of their parents. His brother's house was literally right next door. I was definitely drawn to his coming from a big, close family. And, let's be honest, it was a relief to know that we'd have a lot of backup when the baby came. We would need it.

I was an only child, which had its pros and cons. Growing up, everything was about me, me, and me. My parents spoiled me as best they could. I was their pride and joy, and you bet your ass I loved every second of it. But I always felt alone. I used to beg my mom to adopt another baby from Chile so I could have someone to play with. I had friends, don't get me wrong. Companions were available. But meeting up with a kid on the block on a sunny day wasn't the same as having a sister or brother to hang out with on rainy days when I was stuck in the house. I fantasized about what it'd be like to have a younger sibling I could guide through life and tell how to do important things like dress Barbies and manipulate our parents. (One part charm, one part begging, one part whining, plus a dash of real tears.)

I grew up watching reruns of *The Brady Bunch* and *The Partridge Family* after school. Despite the mega corniness of those shows, being part of a big family looked like a lot of fun, especially getting to wear those matching ridic outfits. The kids might've annoyed each other. And there were a lot of fights. But they were never lonely, never bored. They backed each other up when it mattered. Only siblings can truly appreciate their parents' quirks. Besides parents, only siblings grow up alongside you. You share memories and experiences. It's a unique relationship. My parents gave me everything, and I love them to death for it. But I missed having that brother or sister connection. I think that's why I wanted to have a lot of kids myself. My children would get what I never got to have. It's always go big or go home with me. Even though I didn't know much about living in a big family, I thought, *Fuck it, I want* The Brady Bunch.

Our housing situation settled, I had to go to work. That winter, I moved into a converted firehouse apartment in Jersey City to film *Snooki & JWOWW* Season One. Much as I loved my Booboo and was happy that MTV gave Jenni and me a spin-off, I couldn't get into filming. All I wanted was to be back home and sob hormonally on Jionni's shoulder. It was freezing that winter, and my pregnancy padding wasn't going to keep me warm like my new fiancé. Plus, disgusting pregnancy symptoms had kicked in.

The first to hit was sheer exhaustion. I had to force myself to get out of bed every day. My head was foggy, like I'd just woken up from a coma. The only thing that kept me awake was unrelenting queasiness. I was fortunate not to puke my guts up every five minutes like some pregnant ladies. I had the sick stomach, minus the relief of vomiting. I lived on the verge of it, though. When I ran to the bathroom, I leaned over, but nothing came up. I'd punch the bowl in frustration: "Screw you, toilet!" Cursing at plumbing: A side effect of pregnancy you don't hear about.

Tired, nauseated, foggy. I'd had that cruel combo before. It felt just like a wicked hangover with an Ambien drip. I stopped drinking, yet had the worst hangover of my life with no sign of it letting up? The irony wasn't lost on me. I was so not laughing about it.

Morning sickness? Try morning, afternoon, and evening sickness in a grinding cement mixer with intense hunger pains. At dinnertime, I was torn between the urge to yak, or to eat a yak. My mouth was perpetually full of saliva from thinking about food, or full of that acidy pre-puke drool.

In this hangover-y horror, I had cameras in my face 24/7.

The original concept for *Snooki & JWOWW* was for Jenni and me to have one last fling before we both settled down with our boyfriends. MTV hoped the show would be episode after episode of tipsy, sloppy *Jersey Shore* craziness moved fifty miles north. The producers wanted us, basically, to destroy Jersey City, getting into trouble from start to finish, and leaving scorched burn marks on the street when we left. You should have seen their faces when I told them I was pregnant! They were like, "Get me re-write, ASAP!" I felt for them. It would be hard to make the show fun when one of the "stars" couldn't be the cocktail swilling, hard partying drunk her fans expected. I wasn't that girl anymore. We had to do a different kind of show.

I've got to give the producers credit for rolling with the punches.

We all had to adjust to the sudden change. So, logically, the show would be about that adjustment. It's reality, after all.

On the very first episode, I told Jenni what was going on, saying, "I'm engaged." I started with that to get one shocker out the way before I let loose the even bigger news.

Her reaction was, "No, you're not. That ring isn't real." She was pissed off that I got engaged before her, even though she was five years older than me. She thought of me like a little sister. Little sisters don't get engaged first.

"We had a reason to get engaged," I continued. "Jionni asked me to get married because . . . I'm pregnant."

Her jaw nearly crashed through the floor. It was a lot to take in, although she had to have noticed I'd put on a few pounds. She probably thought that was just winter padding. But still. You tell a friend you're pregnant, you want her to jump up and down and scream, "Congrats!" You want her to throw out baby names and ask if she can hold your hair while you barf.

Jenni was in shock. I knew she reacted that way out of concern for me, and probably for my baby. She told me later she wasn't sure I was ready for motherhood, and if I could handle the demands of filming while pregnant. This was her show, too. We were in it together, for better or preggers. She wouldn't quit or walk off. But she was obviously worried about it, and worried about the changes in my life.

The doubt in her eyes? I felt it, too.

I wasn't sure I was ready to be a mom either. I wasn't one of those women who saw a baby and started drooling. I thought kids were sticky, loud, annoying brats to be avoided in airports and supermarkets. I'd see one coming and think, *Ewww, get away from me!* Thank God Jionni was great with kids. He had seventeen first cousins and a handful of nieces and nephews. He coached wrestling. He babysat one of his nephews every day at lunchtime. I was an only child and don't have cousins. I'd changed one diaper in my life and nearly puked. In several months, I'd be elbow deep in diapers. Holy crap.

Life threw me a curve ball—a sperm ball. The timing wasn't great— for life or the show. The next eight weeks of filming would be rough. But they'd be a blip on the radar. The baby was going to be around (knock on wood) for the rest of my life. I knew Jenni would feel excited about the baby and that she'd love the peanut like her own. She just had to wrap her mind around it.

"Will you be the godmother?" I asked.

That snapped her out of her speechless trance. "Of course!" she said, and gave me a tight, boob-crushing hug. I almost cried—from how much it hurt my swollen tits. (Jenni's implants are kind of hard.) I knew she was really happy for me. But there was something funky left in the air—no, not only the smell of fart. It was the first season of our spin-off. It was supposed to be a blow out. My pregnancy was like pouring ice water into a hot tub.

"I promise I'll be fun," I told her, and meant it. I wasn't going to let pregnancy ruin our good time. I thought I could be my same old self, minus alcohol, plus a huge belly. Just because I was pregnant didn't mean I had to be a boring loser. I was still me, after all, only with a mini-me growing inside.

Which was totally stupid and naïve to think. I had no idea then how much pregnancy would affect my body and mind.

That was the general opinion from all of our friends. "You don't know what you're getting yourself into," they said. "Babysitting isn't the same." Not that I'd ever been a babysitter either.

Yes, we were clueless. But no more so than other first-time parents. Everyone goes into parenting blind. I think this is why pregnancy lasts so long. It takes a good nine months for the future mom and dad—and everyone in their lives—to get adjusted to the fact that a baby is really and truly coming.

(As it turned out, the doubters were right. We didn't know what we were getting ourselves into. But they were also wrong. You don't need to know what you're doing beforehand. In fact, it's better not to know. That way, you won't freak out when things don't go down the way they're "supposed" to. Going in blind is the best way to see parenting clearly. Ignorance = bliss. Totally true.

Since clubs and bars were out for filming, we had to come up with creative alternatives for funny scenes. Jenni and I filmed in a pet store, in a baby clothing store, at a psychic's, and at the doctor's office. We went shopping and out to restaurants. We shot at the firehouse loft and at Jionni's parents' house.

Still with me? You haven't fallen asleep yet? That was how I felt while filming the entire season. In the end, we made it work. We managed to cobble together some hilarious and intense moments. Highlights of the season for me were dyeing Jenni's dogs pink and purple, taking Jionni and Roger to Lucky Cheng's in Manhattan to see a drag show, and my first sonogram (more on that later).

Jenni and I dragged around two dolls that looked, cried, and pooped like real babies to see how tough it was to care for an actual human infant. We dressed them up in swag outfits. I stayed up all night "feeding" the doll. I really wanted to prove to myself that I could do it, no matter how tired I was. I was up anyway because I had to pee every ten minutes. I'd never peed so much in my life. Urinary tract infections have nothing on pregnancy bladder. Most women don't accidentally pee their pants until the third trimester, but this bitch was self-wet from sneezing, coughing, blowing her nose, and laughing too hard. Forget the Real Baby. I was the one who needed a Pampers.

In nearly every clip of the show or any photo taken of me during filming, I looked depressed. I wear my heart on my face. I was miserable! No matter what or where we were filming, I had to run to the bathroom. Due to pregnancy exhaustion, I dragged myself through every day. I pounded bagels and cream cheese to stop the queasiness, which made it worse in a way. Every night, I'd finish all my dinner and then point at Jenni's plate. "You gonna eat that? Because I will."

"What *aren't* you gonna eat?" she asked.

Exactly. It was a weird combination of feeling starving *and* like a fat slob at the same time. I'd sit down at the table, hungry enough to eat a cow—and then I'd eat the whole herd. I polished off jars of jelly with a spoon. I'd slurp down an entire pineapple by myself. After every meal, a food baby grew on top of the fetus. My little offspring probably liked swimming in the yummy taste of spaghetti and marinara sauce, but I felt horrible and huge. I'd heave myself up from the table, stumble to the couch with crumbs and food stains on my shirt, belch, fart, wet myself with pee, and then fall asleep with my mouth open. Sexy! And all of it caught on camera.

I didn't crave specific foods until later, but I hated things right away. I got insta-queasy from the smell of eggs and . . . *pickles*. The food pregnant women are supposed to lust for, my favorite food of all time, suddenly made me sick. Pregnancy turned loves into hates, and hates into loves. It was just an upside-down world. If I thought about mourning my pickle love, I'd have to run to the bathroom to dry heave. Again, *sexy*!

The absolute worst part, though, was gas. It felt like someone stuck an air pump into my navel and inflated my bowels like an air mattress. An alien was growing in my belly and would later emerge whole from my vagina. Fine. I accepted that. Why this process produced *so much* gas, I will never understand.

I was terrified of getting pregnancy hemorrhoids, which I heard was a fate worse than death. Sitting down with a golf ball shoved up my ass would give new meaning to the phrase "rhoid rage." Apparently, hemorrhoids grew from pushing too hard when pooping. To avoid that, I would camp out on the toilet and just wait for the shit to slide out without bearing down. Yeah, it took a while. And considering how much I was eating, there was a lot of waiting involved. And a lot of farting. I never forced my farts out, either. If anything, I suppressed them on camera and whenever I was with Jionni. Call me old fashioned (I dare you), but I don't think it's sexy to fart the alphabet in front of my fiancé. My gas relief needs also sent me running for the bathroom, along with peeing, and dry heaving, and the shits. When pregnant, ladies, you will get to know every inch of your bathroom intimately. Every water stain on the ceiling. Every crack in the paint. The order of the bottles lined up on the shelf. I could draw a picture of that firehouse bathroom from memory, but it might give me nightmares.

This was my life. I wallowed on the toilet or the couch, feeling like Pizza the Hut, desperately missing Jionni—and stone cold *sober*.

I really was at a breaking point when Jenni suggested we get a change in scenery and head down to Cancun, Mexico, in March. My old friend Ryder and another girl were going to come along. I agreed to go on the trip with mixed feelings. It would take me even farther away from Jionni. And what was the point of going to Mexico without tequila? On the other hand, getting out of freezing New Jersey and away from that freakin' bathroom—and into a brand new bathroom—seemed like a good idea. I forgot that it was Spring Break. On the plane down, I realized, *Holy crap, a million college girls in tiny bikinis are going to be crawling all over the beach like sand crabs while I flop around like a whale.*

From the minute I stepped off the plane, I knew it was a mistake. Jenni and Ryder wanted to hit the beach first thing. They tied on string bikinis. I put on my fat-lady caftan. It was a pretty caftan, purple and floral. Perfect for the beach. But I didn't feel comfortable taking it off with all those sexy bodies around me. My friends ordered margaritas. I got a seltzer with lime. They wanted to hit up hotties. I was engaged and pregnant, aka, the opposite of DTF. They were slurping away on margaritas, laughing, and acting crazy.

When you're sober, drunk people are really annoying. Now I could see why people were annoyed by me for all those years.

Although I was sharing a suite with my best friends, I felt completely isolated. I asked at one point if Cancun was an island, and they made fun of me for that. Hey, I knew Mexico wasn't an island. It just felt like I was alone on one. Jenni and Ryder got pissed off at me for whining about my fat pregnancy ass the entire time. It might've been selfish of me to wet blanket their fun. But in my hormone-laced brain, it seemed like they were rubbing my face in what I couldn't do. I was resentful. They lost patience with me. Fun. Meh.

I couldn't break free from that miserable mindset. I tried to snap myself out of it by going to a club. The girls were doing shots and dancing. Some douchebag elbowed Jenni in the eye, and a fight started. I could have been more sympathetic that she got hit in the face. But all I could think about was my baby and that a club was no place for a pregnant woman.

"God forbid I get punched in the stomach and have a miscarriage!" I said to her, while she was holding her just-smacked face. Maybe it wasn't the ideal moment to complain about my own safety.

Pregnancy forces you to see the world through fetus-shaped glasses. Everything I said, thought, did, and ATE was a reaction of my condition. I was obsessed, but not by choice. My body made me obsess. And that affected every moment of the trip. I couldn't even go to a restaurant without the pregnancy taking over my brain. Looking at a menu, half the items made me feel sick, and half weren't healthy for the baby. My friends were smoking and knocking back shots, and it made me depressed. I didn't crave alcohol and cigarettes at all—until I was stuck at a table watching Jenni and Ryder sucking them down. Even fun activities sapped my energy. We went swimming with dolphins, which was cool. But afterwards, when my friends wanted to go to the bar, I had to take a nap.

There was a strange day in Cancun when we went to a gator zoo. I brought Crocadilly, my fave stuffed alligator, which was such a bizarre impulse. Because of the pregnancy, I couldn't do all the things I thought of as "adult." I guess I regressed into a child myself, lugging around a stuffed animal for comfort. My friends treated me like a big annoying baby anyway.

Jenni said, "Pregnancy is not a handicap."

Bullshit! A handicap is something that prevents you from functioning like a normal person. Okay, so pregnancy is temporary, and by choice (or by accident, whatever). It's not like being paralyzed or having a broken leg. Obviously, I wasn't going to park my car in handicapped spaces. But I did feel like I couldn't function like a normal woman. Back in New Jersey, it didn't seem so bad. But in Cancun, every time I turned around, there was something I couldn't do.

The only times I felt happy in Mexico were with the dolphins and at the zoo. I could relate to the animals. The humans? Everyone made me furious. I like being the center of attention. When I feel ignored, I take it to heart more than other people might. Even if I didn't have homicidal hormones coursing through me, I would have been upset by my friends' treatment. It wasn't an ego thing, me bitching that the spotlight wasn't on me. Not at all. It felt like I'd been excluded.

When the girls went off to drink and party and left me behind, I cried on the phone to my dad. He calmed me down. When I hung up, I had a cool realization. One day, the baby in my belly might feel bad on a trip to Mexico and call me to calm her or him down. My baby would need someone to make him feel better, and that person would be me. I wasn't really alone in that hotel room. I had my family with me, literally, in my belly.

Don't get me wrong. I was still really pissed at my friends. But it made me feel a lot better to widen my view of life. They were headed for the club; I was moving in a different direction entirely. Yes, I wished my friends were more sympathetic about what I was going through. But some sacrifices and bumps were to be expected when expecting. I was creating a human life here! That was a huge deal. Some things would have to be put aside until the job was done. The physical and emotional changes were beyond my control. I would have to roll with them.

Wiping my tears in that hotel room, I made my peace with the fact that, for another six months, I was going to have a hair-trigger temper and mood swings. I'd have to drag my fat, tired ass around, annoy my family and friends, feel super sensitive and scared, and hate how my body changed. I would look in the mirror and feel like crying. I'd be bloated, exhausted, and miserable. I wouldn't be happy, but I would try to accept being unhappy.

And when it was all over, I'd have a baby . . . that I had no clue what to do with or how to raise. What the hell had I gotten myself into?

Chapter 3

It's a Meatball!

───oʃo───

When I was twenty weeks pregnant, I had my first sonogram. It was the second major test to see if the baby was okay. I don't know how I would have reacted if the fetus weren't developing right. Like all expectant moms, I imagined some nightmare situations. But I tried to push them out of my mind as quickly as possible. It's not productive or purposeful to agonize about worst-case scenarios. My heart goes out to anyone who has to make tough choices as the result of early pregnancy testing. It's impossible to know how you'd react unless you were actually facing it. Things do go wrong. Nature isn't reliable. When we found out our baby was healthy, it was a tidal wave of relief.

Jionni met Jenni and me at the doctor's office. The ob-gyn was Jionni's mom's doctor. And his sister's and his aunt's. He knew my in-laws' vaginas inside out. It felt good to keep it in the family, and to have my best friend and fiancé with me.

I lay back on an exam room table during the knuckle-biter bitch of a test. The technician lifted my shirt and covered my belly with K-Y jelly. Lube! Were we going to get frisky, or do the sonogram? Then she put a sensor wand that glowed blue on my stomach and rubbed it around.

The probe thing sent sound waves—so high-frequency humans can't hear them, but I bet a bunch of poodles started howling in an alley nearby—into my body. The waves bounced off my organs. The same probe (love the word "probe"—it makes me think of aliens and anuses) received the echoes, which traveled up through the cable into the computer. The computer analyzed the distance between the echoes (do not ask me to go into better details about how the hell *that* works), and an image appeared on the monitor.

"That's your baby," said the sonographer. On the screen, a little half-moon-shaped peanut with skinny legs appeared.

Jenni said, "It looks like a shrimp!" Uh, yeah, it did. Like mother, like father, like shrimp.

My first reaction was to say, "Eww," as in, *The hell? What kind of freaky weird parasite thing is that?* I covered my mouth with my hand and felt like I might throw up. Then again, I always felt like I might throw up. Right there on the screen, I could see the fetus stretching and doing backflips. But I hadn't felt a single flutter yet. For a second,

I didn't believe the fetus was actually inside me. We could make out a bunch of body parts. A foot. The leg. The profile and spine. No sign of the gender yet. It was too early to tell.

The sonographer told us everything looked good. The baby was fine, and proportional. I'd been worried for nothing, but that was a good first lesson on becoming a mom. A mother worries about her kids from the second she pees on a stick until the day she dies. Today at least, I could relax. The baby was healthy. It had all its parts and was growing well and according to schedule. Jionni beamed with pride. Jenni just stared with her mouth open. Until she saw the baby on the monitor, I didn't think she really believed, in her heart of hearts, that I was going to be a mom. I don't know if I did, either, until that moment.

Then we heard the heartbeat. A dull thump-thump muffled by the amniotic fluid filled the room. I reached up for Jionni's arm, smiling ear to ear. I wondered if we could hear the baby burp or fart, too, if it made a loud one. But I was so blown away by what I saw and heard that I forgot to ask.

I started to cry, a total involuntary emotional explosion. Happy tears! Freaked out tears. Amazed tears. I also started giggling, which I always did when nervous and excited. My baby was strong. It was chugging along inside me. In another twenty weeks, it would come out and rip my vagina to the butthole. And then, my massacred crotch and I would be a mom. The sonogram was proof that the pregnancy was genuinely happening. No joke. My wild child was doing cartwheels in my uterus right now, while I watched.

We got our first ever baby picture. I thought about sending it around with the subject line, "It's an Alien Parasite!" We walked out of there on Cloud 19, way higher than Cloud 9. The huge hurdle was cleared, and I felt more committed than ever to this incredible, scary turn my life had taken.

Our next sonogram was a month later. By then, I was living in Seaside Heights, filming *Jersey Shore* Season Six. I brought my roomies Sammi, Deena, and Jenni along for that appointment. Jionni was really excited that day. We would be able to tell if the meatball was a girl or a boy.

Sammi and Deena hadn't seen a sonogram before, and they were stunned by how cool it was to look inside one person's body and see another human body. I was my own Russian nesting doll.

"Definitely a boy," said the sonographer.

"Where?!" I yelled. She pointed to the baby braciola. "That's the penis? That whole thing?"

It was huge. You'd have to be blind to miss it. I thought our baby's penis was as long as a third leg. Even the doctor said that he was large and in charge.

Jionni had wanted a boy. Seeing his son's penis for the first time is, apparently, a major moment for any expectant DILF. Jionni puffed up like it was his own penis we were all cheering about. Honestly? I sort of wanted a girl, just to have a mini-me to dress up. But learning our baby's sex was a fantastic feeling. Hello, Mommy's Boy! I started to imagine a combination of our features on a baby boy's face. He would be so cute! I didn't care if he looked more or less like either of us. As long as he had Jionni's butt.

Here's Jionni

It was exciting to find out we were having a boy. I was happy about getting that out of the way first. It means a lot. I grew up playing sports with my dad and brothers. I still play a lot and coach wrestling. I know a girl can play sports, too. And I will love a girl just as much when we have one. I know Nicole wanted a girl. But I really wanted a son. He'll be my little man. I can see us throwing a football and hitting golf balls together one day. Can't wait.

I wonder if the baby knew my first thought was, *Not a girl*. While we were watching him on the screen, he lifted his hand and raised his middle finger at us. He flipped us off! He seemed to be waving it in our direction. Maybe he was trying to sleep and he had enough of the megahertz sound waves that only dogs, whales, and fetuses can hear. I loved him even more. Seeing that finger, I thought proudly, "He's one of us."

Jionni and I needed to choose a strong name to hang on that massive penis. We briefly considered the name Tripod. Kidding. We definitely had no intention of giving him an object name like Apple or Lamp Shade. (Why do celebrity parents do this? As if Blanket wouldn't have a hard enough life just being Michael Jackson's son?) We wanted a traditional Italian name, so we flipped through our mental list of names we'd heard and liked. Jionni came up with Lorenzo. For a middle name, we chose Dominic, after my deceased uncle, as a tribute to my dad. Bingo! We would christen our baby Lorenzo Dominic LaValle. Italian and sexy.

As soon as we gave him a name, we decided Lorenzo would have my outgoingness and heart and Jionni's athleticism and looks. We wanted the best for our boy. I couldn't wait to meet the little dude.

We got one last look at Enzo in utero. It was at the very end of the pregnancy, a 3D image that was as detailed as any regular black and white photo. He had hair, chubby cheeks, my lips, and Jionni's nose. Our alien offspring finally looked human. I watched my baby yawn in real time, as if a camera had been snaked inside me. He was so big by then, I swear I could feel the yawn as it was happening. It made me want to yawn myself. I loved him so much already.

As exciting as the sonograms were, they started to piss me off. Enough with sound waves already! I wanted to see my baby the flesh.

Chapter 4

MILF *in Training*

As soon as I first heard the term MILF (mother I'd like to fuck, or basically, a hot older woman), I wanted to be one. I'd be a MILF, married to a DILF (same thing for guys), and we'd have adorable tan babies. Four of them, three boys and one girl. So, when I found out I was pregnant, I'd already been a MILF-in-training, at least mentally, for years. I had a checklist of MILF must-haves: looking good at all times, keeping your weight down during pregnancy, perfect hair, nails, and makeup, even in the labor and delivery room.

I thought it was possible to act the part all the time. But after I got pregnant, I realized that wasn't going to happen. I couldn't be a MILF one hundred percent of the time if I felt like a fat, bloated slob ninety percent of the time. I had to work around my growing belly. In the past, dressing with style was a huge part of feeling pretty for me. How the hell would I pull it off when I felt like a whale?

As it turned out, pregnancy was the mother of invention. I had to figure out a new way of dressing. I didn't have a choice. None of my clothes fit. I had to lower the bar on expectation whenever I stepped in front of the mirror. Since I look in the mirror and take selfies a thousand times a day, I had a lot of mental adjustments to make. The only thing that kept me on the right side of disgusted, though, was determination. Doing the best I could with what I had to work with helped me think more highly of myself, especially when I felt like dung. Getting dressed, shopping, planning outfits, and organizing my closet was a distraction from dry hurls and gas attacks, which in itself was a gift from God.

I was particularly style challenged by the timing of my pregnancy. My due date was early September 2012. July and August were the hottest on record. Temperatures were over a hundred degrees for days on end. I couldn't hide in bulky sweaters. If I wore too much of *anything,* I would have fainted from heat stroke. Cute sundresses and flowing tops saved me. I don't know how I would have gotten through the heat without them.

The day of my baby shower was a scorcher. Jionni got so dizzy and dehydrated playing golf, he had to go to the emergency room (he was fine). Despite the heat, I felt beautiful in a black-and-white sexy sundress that showed off my boobs, and six-inch-high black sandals.

I think I got them at Mandee for, like, $30.

Turnsout, I didn't buy a single piece of maternity clothing. I checked out some of the stores, but nothing was cute. It was all so boring and beyond expensive. I guess the logic is that they have to charge more for all that extra fabric. Bullshit. Expectant moms are at the store's mercy. They double the price because their customers are desperate and think they have no other choice but to pay the Mommy Tax markups. A hundred bucks for a plain black t-shirt dress that made me look a bowling ball? Ridiculous.

You will never see me spending thousands of dollars on designer clothes. Paying sky-high prices for a wardrobe I'd use for a few months only? The definition of insanity. For the duration of my pregnancy, I went the cheap route, making the rounds at old faves like Bebe or Mandee. I pulled off the rack whatever looked cool, just in a bigger size. Ordinarily, I have the body of a twelve-year-old (if she had boobs). So I could fit my Buddha belly into a regular size L. I didn't even need to go up to an XL. Weird irony: At my pre-pregnancy weight, I couldn't always find clothes small enough for me. So I actually had more options pregnant than I did before.

The bigger I got, the bolder my style. When I had only a little bump, I entered my Poncho Phase. Belly-hugging clothes made me look fat, not quite knocked up. Plus I was scared constrictive clothes would strangle my baby. Women could faint from wearing corsets. You could sort of see how a bandage club dress would compress the fetus and make it grow into a weird shape. I wasn't going to risk that. (Obviously, that's not a real danger. Just pregnancy brain paranoia. Unless you're wearing a belt cinched tight as a tourniquet, your baby is protected no matter how tacky you dress.) Hopefully, in the near future, I'll design hot clothes for pregnant ladies of all sizes. In the meantime, I had to improvise. Around month six or seven, when it was clear that I was pregnant, I started wearing clingy clothes. I thought, *I can keep trying to hide, or I can show off my bump proudly.* I was happiest with my style when I was showing off.

So what did I rely on? I could not live without my:

Ponchos. A poncho is like a tent you throw over your shoulders. It hides everything underneath. It was the perfect solution to the "Is she pregnant, or just a legit blimp?" stage. My ponchos always had vibrant prints. Patterns do a good job of masking bulges and bumps, too.

Leggings. I got a dozen pairs of leggings—denim, faux leather, in colors and patterns—in bigger sizes and stretchy fabrics. The best had drawstring waistbands and expanded along with my belly. I didn't wear pants with a button or zipper for about eight months. Stretch waists are dangerous when you're not knocked up. But when you are? Life savers! I lived in mine.

Harem pants. I avoid harem pants when not pregnant, because they remind me of clowns. But for the second trimester, harem pants were the perfect camouflage for the growing tummy. I put a belt right under my boobs to define a "waist," and felt fly in those magic carpet pants.

Wrap dresses. No buttons and zippers with wrap dresses. They're designed to be adjustable around the middle. The only way a wrap dress would get too small was if it didn't overlap across my belly. Fortunately, that didn't happen. The bow in front just kept getting smaller and smaller. I had to tie it right under my boobs in a knot by the end.

Headbands. My signature look included a silk flower headband or a cute bow. Putting a topper on my look added a pop of color to any outfit. During pregnancy, it also drew attention up, up, all the way to my hair (which looked freakin' awesome thanks to the vitamins and hormones). The bigger my stomach, the larger my flowers and bows. I just felt prettier knowing that the focus of my outfit was on my head, not my belly.

Cute tops. By the third trimester, there was no chance of defining a waist. So I put on flowing blouses with leggings. I gravitated toward bright colors like red and orange. They flattered my skin tone (although

I wasn't as tan as usual; no products while preggers). The color made me feel happy, too. A few of my tops were borderline hippie-ish. Boho wasn't my thing . . . until I tried it, and then I really got into it. Pregnancy didn't only stretch my belly, but it expanded my style range.

Stretch! Fabrics that give are a pregnant lady's bestie. You can get pretty much anything in stretch materials these days: tops, jeans, and dresses. I wore stretchy t-shirts and sundresses, usually in bright colors and prints. Speaking of . . .

Prints and shine. Even when I wore black, I made sure it had sparkle and shine, like studs, beading, or sequins. My fallback print will always be leopard. I even wore a t-shirt that had a giant leopard on the front. As long as I wore my spots, I felt strong and fierce. Rawr!!

Jackets are the finishing piece that pulls an outfit together. My shoulders and arms didn't get fat, so I could shop for jackets while pregnant that I could keep for after. I had to leave them open—all the better for showing off the dress underneath. Even with a blazer, I amped it up with sequins. Everyone knows that if you're in a black leather jacket, you *will* feel tough and sexy. Mine gave me an instant mood swing in the right direction.

Drawers. Gawd. Forget trying to be a sexy little thing in thongs. I swear, I told myself early on that I was going to be hot and sexy throughout the nine months. But once my belly popped and I turned gigantic, it was all downhill, as far as underwear is concerned. I packed away all the sexy thongs and booty shorts, because they wouldn't fit over my leg.

The first time I shopped for pregnancy bras and underwear, I was mortified. Everything looked like something my great-great-grandmother would wear. But these old lady undergarments were the most comfortable panties I have ever worn, like a silky diaper. I'm talking grandma panties that covered my whole ass and part of my legs and pulled all the way up to over my boobs. They were so big, they could pass for a mini dress.

The bras were comfortable, too! They are intimidating to look at, though. The cup sizes were literally the size of my head, and the style was hideous. But they did a good job of holding up my big milk melons—and I needed the support.

Heels. My standby style pick-me-up has always been heels. I know everyone has an opinion on wearing heels during pregnancy. When I was in six-inch wedges, some woman came up to me and said, "Heels will hurt the baby!" Bitch, get real. If you know how to wear them, heels won't hurt a fly, let alone a baby. I happen to be a pro. I've been rocking six-inchers since age fourteen. During pregnancy, I wore comfortable heels I could balance in, like platforms and wedges. Even my pumps had a chunky, stable heel.

And I needed the lift. As soon as I slipped on a nice shoe, I felt so much better. Pretty, even. During the last couple of months of pregnancy, when I was mistaken for a walrus on the beach, I needed to raise my spirits. As long as I could fit cool shoes on my bloated feet, I thought, *I'm doing it and no one can tell me different.* I wore three-inchers until the ninth month. I lived in my Jeffrey Campbell platforms until the fifth month.

Slippers. When it was time to *really* relax, I put on my cute slippers, threw my hair into a pony, shrugged on a leopard print silk robe, grabbed my ice cream, and sank into the couch. Yes! The Chillin' Hour, just like the end of a non-pregnant day, but times a hundred to take the load off. Slippers go on, stress disappears.

Style was only half of the expectant MILF formula. You can put on the cutest dress, but if your face doesn't look good, you might as well be wearing a garbage bag. You must wear makeup. When you're dolled up, you will feel glamorous, even while farting, gagging, and peeing yourself. You can be a gassy bloated slob, or a *classy* gassy bloated slob. Choose classy.

Every morning, I woke up and put on blush. Instantly, I felt a little better emotionally no matter how shitty I felt physically. My mommy training included a lot of lifting of the lipgloss wand. I kept up with my false eyelash routine, too. Why should my lashes be smaller if my belly was bigger? It made no sense. If anything, I wanted more lash. I went through mascara by the case. As long as that part of me was flawless, I could deal with what wasn't.

Unfortunately, my skin during pregnancy was blotchy, zitty, and puffy. A trifecta of horrible. I used a lot of concealer. Because I wasn't tanning at all—bed, sun, or spray—my skin got lighter and lighter. I had to adjust my concealer shade a few times. I made up for being pale by lavishing moisturizer on my skin every day.

What disgusted me the most, though, were the breakouts. Was I a 24-year-old woman, or a 13-year-old girl going through puberty? The zits were angry, gross, and legion—and not only on my face. They sprouted up like the plague all over my chest. A village of pimples made a nice home in the valley of my boobs during the three hottest days of summer. Jesus God. Beyond not okay! I tried to get rid of it by using face masks repeatedly on my chest. When it got really dry and crackling, I slathered on moisturizer. Eventually, I conquered zit village, but talk about yuck.

The only positive beauty change during pregnancy was that my hair grew thick and shiny from all the vitamins and hormones. It got so thick, straightening it took forever. If I flat ironed at home, it would take hours. But I enjoyed it. The process was hypnotic and really did calm and soothe. Around month four, I did my research about all-natural safe-while-pregnant hair color. My stylist used an ammonia-free lightener and all-organic color. I went from having dark brown hair with red streaks to black hair with blond tips for summer. I also put in Barbie-long extensions, just for fun. Along with my hair, I lavished attention on my nails, which also grew like crazy. I got mani-pedis about once a week.

I did what I could do to make myself feel better. If that meant spending two hours flat ironing my Barbie extensions, fine. It's the pregnant lady's prerogative to pamper herself. She'll be elbow deep in Pampers soon enough.

Chapter 5

Whale Sex

I went to college to become a veterinary technician, aka the person who holds the animal while the doctor does all the medical stuff. While I was a student, I wrote a long research paper on the Mating Rituals and Habits of the Blue Whale, the largest animal to have ever existed on Earth. Some fun factoids: A male blue whale penis is ten feet long and as big around as a basketball. The female's vulva lips are as long as helicopter propellers with nipples at the ends for feeding calves. The male and female bang in warm water. After a year of gestation, the baby comes out fluke first, weighing 6,000 pounds, about the same size as my SUV.

I never found out some important information, such as whether or not blue whales smush during pregnancy, if the calf is emotionally scarred that his parents were knocking fins while he was in utero, if the female whale has orgasms, or if it's true that dribbled-out whale sperm makes the ocean salty. Sadly, experts just don't know all that much about the sex lives of blue whales.

Given that our DNA is, like, 99 percent the same (give or take a chromosome or two), and that I felt like a whale during pregnancy, my sex life during that time might fill in some holes regarding these majestic and mysterious sea creatures. Marine biologists: Get out your iPads and start taking notes on the mating habits of the "Tan Whale:"

The male has a ten-inch-long penis that's as big around as a baseball. You're welcome, Jionni.

Immediately after conception, the female has vivid, kinky wet dreams. Oh, yeah, baby! This was a major bonus of the early months. I had crazy, sexy dreams. I only wish I could remember what, or who, they were about. Didn't matter. My subconscious was literally fucking with me. I'd have an orgasm that was so powerful and intense, it would wake me up out of a dead sleep. My eyes would fly open, and I'd gasp for breath, my legs shaking. I read somewhere that the baby can feel the mother's orgasm. I guess it gets rattled around from the spasms. Does it know what's going on? Maybe it sees rainbows and unicorns? Um, awkward.

During the first trimester, both genders enjoy increased desire. We realized I was pregnant a few days into the New Year. Looking back at our sex life in November and December, we were getting it in like we were trying to conceive. The holidays were a raging smutfest. I thought it was because we were just in a good place romantically. But now I think it was because I was juicing on hormones. I probably put out a chemical signal to Jionni's lizard brain that I was carrying his fetus, so he wanted me more. I was climbing the walls to get to him. I just couldn't keep my hands off him. Once we knew we were pregnant, our drive kicked into an even higher gear. It was a huge turn on for me to be future parents together. Plus, I wasn't showing yet. I could do all the positions without feeling self-conscious.

During the second trimester, the female's sex drive decreases rapidly. When I started showing in the sixth month, desire turned off. I went from massively turned on to completely switched off. It didn't have anything to do with Jionni's behavior or sex appeal. He was the same damn handsome Italian stallion he always had been. But he'd come at me with his junk, and I'd slap it away, screaming, "Get that thing away from me!" and then run for the bathroom. My stomach was constantly queasy. Sex only churned up my sick stomach. I was exhausted, in pain, and inflated with gas, fetus, and fluid. The last thing I needed was something else shoved in me. As my belly grew, it felt like my vagina shrank. There wasn't any room to maneuver in there. Sex got really uncomfortable. The only position that didn't feel like being impaled on a stake was side-by-side—spooning position, aka, what old people do when they've been married for twenty years and are too bored and lazy to get on top of each other. Spooning is sweet, I guess. It's cozy. But it is so not hot!

Unfortunately, the male's sex drive increases. I'd always wanted big JWOWW boobies, and when I hit the second trimester, I got them. Before my pregnancy, I always had swollen, sore breasts before my period. Welp, pregnancy boobs put period boobs to shame. They *ached*. When I bumped into something, I'd groan and almost pass out. As painful as they were, they did look ripe and bountiful. I understood why men were fascinated by ginormous breasts just by looking at myself in the mirror. Jionni *loved* them. He grabbed for them every chance he got. I had to boob block him. "You can look all you want, but don't touch!" I yelled. Seriously, the tiniest contact sent a shock of pain through my entire system. I couldn't get comfortable, especially when I needed my beauty rest. Lying on my stomach, they squished. Lying on my side, they squeezed. Lying on my back, *sploosh*. Bras pressed against the soreness. I tried free-boobing it with layers of clothes to keep them somewhat penned in. That made Jionni want me even more.

By the third trimester, the female would rather chew off her own limb than have sex. I would have loved to be like this one pregnant girl who told me smushin' with a cushion was amazing. But I cringed whenever Jionni raised his eyebrows at me. Never thought I'd hate smutting with my man. I did put on a brave face and try to do it a few times toward the end. I would feel okay for about one minute, but then I'd ice over in pain. I would tell him to hurry up and pray it was over quickly. I just didn't feel sexy. Jionni assured me, "You're beautiful. You're as sexy to me now as you always were." My pregnancy paranoia took over, though, and I worried he was lying to me.

We both knew my body changes were temporary. My attitude was, "Let's just wait to have sex until I feel sexy and not like I'm about to explode placenta all over the room. Sex hurts. I'm enormous. I don't want to disappoint you, or turn you off, or get impaled, or have bad associations with being pregnant since I want to do it again three more times. Plus, I have to go pee/poop/fart/eat right now. So let's put your penis away for the next three months."

Here's Jionni

Pregnancy sex? Did we have pregnancy sex? Maybe that one time.

We had a long dry spell. Her attitude was, "Let's not." And my attitude was, "Let's go."

Honestly, I wasn't turned off at all. I didn't care what Nicole looked like. To me, she was the same woman I fell in love with and wanted to marry. My attraction didn't change because her body did. She thought that. I never did. She's my fiancée. She's carrying my child. That attracted me to her. Her boobs were a few sizes bigger. That was definitely a plus.

But if she didn't want to, I wasn't going to push. I was a good sport about it. It was all about Nicole. I really understood. I wasn't happy! But I understood.

He did tell me I was just as beautiful to him as ever, even thirty pounds heavier. But we argued about it. He got sick of telling me that I was still sexy. But I couldn't get enough of hearing it. I was a needy bitch. Any small slight turned into a major fight in a matter of seconds, thanks to hormones.

On top of all that tension, we had a semi-long distance relationship. In March, I was in Jersey City filming *Snooki & JWOWW*. In June and July, I was in Seaside Heights to film *Jersey Shore* season six. Jionni was back in North Jersey. He came to visit me as often as possible. But we got a bit out of sync with each other.

When we were apart, I worried he was looking at and talking to other women. When we were together, I was grouchy and whining.

By the end of pregnancy, the couple shelves sex completely, except for the occasional pity handjob. As a devoted fiancée, there was nothing I wouldn't do for my man (for five minutes). One bit of advice for future dads: Be happy with whatever bones your pregnant girl throws you. Otherwise, take a shower, lather up, and have fun.

Sexually, we got through the pregnancy intact. Even acutely frustrated, Jionni was there for me when I needed him. I was nervous that he'd stopped feeling attracted to me. Not his fault! He did everything right to make me feel appreciated and adored despite the fact that he wasn't getting within ten feet of me. For a few months there, we were just friends. No, not "just" friends. Best friends, without benefits.

Of course, we did get the biggest benefit in the end. The baby benefit.

Chapter 6

Swinger

W omen talk about the pregnancy brain that turns you stupid and forgetful. Mine turned me into a raving maniac. Tears would shoot out of my eyes. My anger would make veins pop on my neck. I was a certified psychopath during my pregnancy. If I wasn't eating, gagging, or propelling myself around the room by ass gas, I was complaining, crying, yelling, or sulking. The crankiness was a surprise. I was so happy about being pregnant, I didn't realize the hormones would take over my brain and make me hate the world. I'd be hyper and happy one minute, and then I'd attack Jionni like a banshee with a machete if he disagreed with me. Or I'd go from sad and crying, to eyes bugging out of my skull in anger, to whimpering for a hug. I was carrying a baby and had turned into an infant . . . or a psycho bitch in need of medication. I wasn't the most emotionally stable person before, but during pregnancy, all restraint was gone.

Here's Jionni

In the early stages, Nicole wasn't so bad. At the end, though, she got needy. She was really milking the pregnancy. I was her slave 24/7. Whatever she wanted to eat, I had to get. Whatever she asked, I would do. I would agree with anything she said. Her farts didn't smell, either. If she got tired or her feet ached, It was my fault. I just didn't argue with her. She was pregnant with our child. It was the least I could do to make her comfortable and be wrong. Being right calmed her—for a few minutes. I didn't let her swings phase me at all. I was committed to doing the best I could for her, even if that meant getting yelled at. I had sympathy for what she was going through. I just had to stick it out until she returned to normal.

After nine months of sobbing and screaming, I'm amazed Jionni still wants to marry me. I have to give my fiancé props. He dealt with my tantrums like a Sensei. It took that much patience to handle me.

I wanted to murder him at least once a day. No reason. Just . . . because I was tired and queasy. Hormones took my emotions hostage. I had no control over how I reacted. I'd never been good at editing my feelings, so it all just came out like a machine gun blast. Jionni was the innocent bystander, in the wrong place at the wrong time.

Here's a typical conversation from around month seven.

Jionni: "What should we have for dinner?"

Nicole: "Why are you always asking me questions? Stop pressuring me!"

Jionni: "I'm sorry. I didn't mean to upset you."

Nicole (crying): "I'm an asshole. I don't know why you put up with me. I don't deserve you."

Jionni (coming toward Nicole to hug her): "No problem. It's all this hormonal shit and . . ."

Nicole: "What are you saying? My feelings aren't real? Fuck you! You don't know what I'm going through!"

Jionni: "Nicole, you're acting like a crazy person."

Then I'd run to the bathroom and sob hysterically like my cat died. My pregnancy had all the tears and fights of a Telemundo soap opera, except that it made no sense at all, and I wasn't hot.

The worst part about being a swinger was the whiplash. My

emotions would turn my head around so fast, I looked (and acted) like the girl in *The Exorcist*. I wrote down in my pink journal, "Be nice to Jionni! Look what he has to deal with!" The more I tried to rein it in, the more out of control I felt. I wasn't just Pregnancy Bipolar, with being up and being down. I was Tripolar or Quadpolar. Up, down, sideways, backwards, diagonal. I couldn't predict where my emotions would go, how they'd change, how quickly I'd go berserk.

One day, Jionni could joke around with me and call me an idiot. I'd laugh and feel so much love for my man that I'd cry for joy. The same exact scenario could take the place the next day, and I'd explode like a volcano, spewing angry lava, leaving nothing but scorched earth behind me. After a couple of incidents like that, Jionni was scared to talk to me at all.

Whenever we discussed the baby, my emotions were on a roller coaster. Sometimes, I'd feel unbearably excited to meet Lorenzo. Other times, I'd be speechless with terror about what kind of mother I'd be. Then I'd feel bottomless sadness for no reason at all. I cried once a day from month four until the end. At one point, I was having lunch with a friend and went from laughing my butt off, to weeping into my plate.

"People are staring," she said self-consciously, glancing around the restaurant.

Yeah, you don't want to be seen in the company of a weepy pregnant lady. Other people will think you are a total bitch for making her cry.

"Who cares if they stare?!!" I yelled. "Sorry to make you feel *uncomfortable*. I wouldn't want you to get *upset* or anything."

She just shook her head at me with pity. "Nicole, I think you're having a legit mental breakdown."

I have a long history with mini-meltdowns. Every month, during PMS, I feel super sensitive and act like a lunatic. My week of being an unpredictable bitch is, in its way, predictable for my friends and family. At the first psycho sign, they know to back away, slowly, with their hands up.

Well, pregnancy was "that time of the month" every day for nine months. And that's if you don't have postpartum depression, which I've heard is like the ninth circle of Hell. That's serious shit, and needs medication. So-called "normal" hormonal breakdowns like mine just had to be endured.

Jionni got used to me saying "I'm sorry!", "Don't hate me," and "I didn't mean it!" If I wasn't crying or yelling, I was apologizing for the horrible things I said. Words would fly out of my mouth before I could stop them—especially if there was any implication I was fat. If Jionni said, "Still hungry?" I'd freak out.

"Are you saying I'm fat?" I'd scream.

"No! I'm . . . I just . . . can I go watch TV upstairs?"

"Oh, God, I'm so sorry! Say you forgive me!"

He'd sigh and say, "I forgive you. But . . . can I still go upstairs?"

I wish I could blame my shaky emotions solely on hormones. But they were triggered by a few different factors, like frustration with my body changes.

I'd read that after the halfway mark, things were supposed to get better before they got a lot worse. You were showing, so people didn't think you were just gigantic. You weren't so huge that you couldn't fit through a store aisle. Morning sickness eased up. During the sixth and seventh month, you were supposed to feel more energy and less exhaustion. That was the myth anyway.

For me, big surprise, the second half of pregnancy just increased all the lousy symptoms. I started to think I wasn't ever going to get a break. My stress doubled down when we started filming Season Six of *Jersey Shore* in Seaside Heights.

I didn't put on a swimsuit or go near the ocean — or a hot tub — for the entire six weeks of filming. I was sure some of the water, bacteria, chemicals, or slut-borne spirochetes would get inside me and deform my baby. That thought alone made me a wreck. I became convinced that just being in the shore house with my roomies was dangerous for the baby. The place was filthy with food left out all over the place, bugs, dogs, dog shit, and about fifteen different kinds of mold and germs. I should have worn a surgical mask just to walk in the door. People don't necessarily classify paranoia as a "mood," but my mind swung in that direction constantly during the summer. I was so afraid of something going wrong, I played it super safe. I moved out of the house and into a bungalow next door where I could sleep and stay clean.

That made me feel safer. But I was still pretty miserable about all the limitations. I was just *round*. I moved at half my normal speed, like a sea mammal flopping awkwardly on land. Every day, I lived in fear someone would see me on the boardwalk and report a manatee sighting.

And I was sober. It was like Cancun all over again, times seven. Being in Seaside for the previous four summers had been all about boozing and partying. We'd drink and dance every night. But being pregnant, I couldn't be around alcohol. My roomies were supportive and they understood. But watching them drink made me crave alcohol. Shots of OJ and pineapple juice weren't as fun as Jäger and

Patrón. I started to really miss what I couldn't have. The closer I got to giving birth, the harder it was to stick to the rules. I did, of course. But man, did I want a drink!

Although there was no chance I'd give into temptation, I thought, *Why test myself?* That meant avoiding my friends, which made me feel isolated. They were still doing what we always did—swilling tequila, getting in fights, hooking up, making fools of themselves. You know, fun. But I couldn't join in. They were NC-17, and I was G-rated. I tried to get in on the action with them, but it felt wrong. A pregnant woman shouldn't go clubbing. She shouldn't crawl home at dawn, or throw punches, or brush her teeth with vodka and pizza. She should put her swollen feet up, eat lots of hydrating watermelon, and take naps. So that's what I did.

Sure, I missed being in the shore house, and doing shore things. But then again, I was glad not to have to get involved in all the craziness, the hangovers, the drama. Pregnancy does make a woman single-minded, even when she's going a million emotions a minute. My entire life had been reduced to one thing: all pregnancy, all the time. I don't blame my roomies for giving me a wide berth— not only because I took up the whole sidewalk.

I was worried they were avoiding me, or bored with me. But it wasn't true. In the end, they threw me a baby shower, brought Jionni into the circle, and made me feel loved and supported. When I did manage to connect with my friends—like when I brought Sammi and Deena to my sonogram and when Jenni and I visited the doctor after she hurt her foot at the club—I felt really happy. But then—whiplash—I'd get sad and sulky. It wasn't only the final season of *Jersey Shore*. For me, it was also the end of an era of my life, and the beginning of a new, foreign, unknown one that scared the shit out of me.

The only thing that I could rely on to always make me feel better? A long, hard fart.

You basically have to give yourself over to being completely out of control. As soon as you stop trying to steer the swings, you can relax and enjoy being a psycho bitch. It helped me to see the positive side of it. I could scream and cry and punch, and people would forgive me. Being pregnant does let you get away with horrible behavior—with good reason, since you didn't do it on purpose. The victims of your swings see you as an innocent, helpless creature that might snap and whine, but she's so cute, you get over it.

Chapter 7

She's Always Right

———✦———

This is Jionni, Nicole's fiancé, aka the Impregnator. Nicole wanted me to write a chapter in the middle of the book for all the guys who have to deal with their pregnant girlfriends and wives. If I had one rule that ruled them all, it was, "She's always right." As long as I kept that in mind, I could talk to Nicole and get through some tense hours, even a whole day, with my nuts attached. If you can make that your mantra—"she's always right . . . she's always right . . ."—nine months of pregnancy won't feel like a decade.

I made a list of other things to constantly remind myself about Nicole during this time. Dads: copy these pages and hang them on the wall. Read them every day.

◆ Mood swings are coming, whether you expect them or not.

◆ No matter how nice and soft you talk to her, you'll always have an attitude.

She's Always Right

◆ Her fuse is short! She gets mad faster. Learn to duck if she throws a phone at you.

◆ If it smells like a fart, 99 percent of the time, it was hers.

◆ Do NOT blame her for the fart smell.

◆ No matter how wrong she is, tell her she's right.

◆ No matter how wrong she says you are, don't get mad.

◆ She will say rude and hurtful things, but she doesn't really mean it.

◆ If you say rude and hurtful things to her, you are in deep shit.

◆ She is the mother of your child. Always care, always be there.

◆ Try to make her smile. Try again. Try harder.

◆ You will gain weight, because you'll eat when she does.
And she eats a lot.

◆ Do NOT point out how much she's eating.

◆ Fights happen. She might apologize a dozen times, or she'll refuse to apologize at all. Either way, bite your lip and do what you can to cheer her up.

◆ Every look you give her is nasty. Every comment is rude.
You're a jerkoff. When she points this out, agree with her.

◆ Whenever you get frustrated, remember it's temporary.
Suck it up.

Baby Bumps

- Having a baby is not an accident or mistake. It's a blessing.

- Make sure your girl knows how much you love her and the baby, and that you'll be at her side until the end.

- If she runs to the bathroom and turns on the water, do NOT go near there.

- Don't knock on the bathroom door and ask if she's all right. Even if she's crying, leave her alone.

- Tell her she's beautiful, but don't go over the top or she'll get mad.

- You take the blame and apologize even if you've done nothing wrong, be sincere (or at least act sincere) so she'll get over whatever she's mad about quickly.

- Laughter is key. It'll change her bad mood and make her happy. Tell her jokes. But beware . . .

- Pregnancy makes you unfunny. Jokes that used to crack her up won't anymore. You need new material.

- Don't act sad or it will bring her down. She needs you to keep her happy.

- If you try to cuddle and got kicked off the couch, just get up, dust off, and move to the other couch.

Chapter 8

The High Price of Gas

A friend told me once, years ago, that gas pains were like contractions. So whenever I had gas, I'd play house and pretend I was going into labor. Well, my girlhood gas pains were *nothing*—gas *pings*—compared to what I experienced when I was actually pregnant. They were worse than contractions! My gas was super premium extra leaded.

I only made it worse by trying to hold in my farts. When I was in bed cuddling my sweetie, the last thing I wanted to do was let out my toxic air. My crying jags and crazy talk were scary enough. I thought my trumpet farts would blast him right out of the relationship. I'd lay there, butt cheeks clamped tight, squeezing that sucker back in, dying in pain, praying he'd fall asleep already so I could let loose—and not shatter the windows when I did.

I know now that I shouldn't have held back. In my next pregnancy, I won't think twice. But with Lorenzo, I did the polite thing of going into the bathroom, turning the water on, and letting those suckers rip in privacy. The pain I had from holding back wasn't worth Jionni's romantic illusions. Better to save all the pain for labor. You want to be as comfortable as possible during these nine months. You're creating human life. For some reason, that process produces enough gas to power the Mars Rover. If you have to fart, THEN FREAKIN' FART! If you have to scream at someone, THEN FREAKIN' SCREAM. If you have to have a mental break down, GO INSANE. You'll feel so much better! Just let it all out, get your relief, have some ice cream, and take a beauty nap.

Around twenty-six weeks, I was out to dinner with Jionni, and I started having intense pains. I was sure they were contractions. It was too early for Braxton Hicks. Having real contractions at this point would be bad. I freaked out. "I'm in premature labor!" I screamed. "Call the doctor!"

We got him on the phone. Sitting there at the table with my food in front of me, I cried, "It's this spasm in my gut." I described the pain in detail.

He said, "Okay, Nicole. You're not in labor. You're not having contractions."

I was in serious agony. "What is it?"

"Gas," he said.

Holy fucking hell! I'd been pinching it back all night. We were in the car together in that closed space. Then we were at a crowded restaurant with people around. I'd been polite and self-conscious, and this was the price. My date was ruined from blocked gas release.

"Listen, Nicole," said the doctor. "It's not good for you to hold it in."

"But the stench . . ."

"As your doctor, I advise you to go to the bathroom, or go outside to the parking lot, and do what you have to do."

If he said so. My prescription: FART. I took his advice. It was a medical necessity. From that point on, instead of worrying about it or even running to the bathroom to unleash, I crop dusted on the spot.

Not to say that giving myself permission to gust at will was the solution to my problem. The plague of my pregnancy took on a new dimension: I was perfectly willing to fart my way to the moon, but it wouldn't come out! I was afraid of bearing down and forcing it, though, because I was deathly afraid of hemorrhoids.

Since growing a fetus takes up so much of the body's energy, all the other systems slow way down, including digestion. So your food moves through you like cement. Gas builds up, and a lot of women suffer with terrible constipation. They really struggle hard to move that shit along. All the strain and pressure on the blood vessels and muscles in the butt causes hemorrhoids. I'd heard it was like having an egg embedded in your ass. Friends of mine have had two or even three of them at a time. The last thing I needed was an Easter egg hunt in my rectum.

Despite my trapped gas and constipation—and the pain that went with them—I would not bear down for fear of hemorrhoids. (I also thought pushing to poop would make Lorenzo fall out into the toilet. You just can't push hard without worrying about shitting out your baby. You're going to think it, even if you know it's not physically possible. Pregnancy defies logic.) I devised a system for pooping. Whenever I started to strain, I did some breathing to calm down. And then I'd try to relax all my muscles. I visualized it just sliding out. I sat there and waited until it did. I logged, as it were, a lot of bathroom time. I probably sat on the toilet more than the couch during the pregnancy.

One really bad night, I had terrible gas and tried to release the toxic cloud, but it was stuck. I pictured it like a pocket of green gas, trapped in a cranny in my intestine. I thought it'd loosen up if I were on the toilet. I sat in there for an hour. This pain was so bad, I went ahead and pushed, the whole time terrified I'd pop a hemorrhoid. My guts felt twisted and locked. I started crying. I just felt completely alone and useless. I thought, "If I can't crap, what *can* I do?" My entire existence and sense of self-worth were wrapped up in not being able to fart. This is what pregnancy can do to a person. It's not about being smart or successful or rich or talented. When a pregnant woman's body goes haywire on hormones and cement shit, at some point, she'll find herself on the toilet, a red ring mark around her ass from sitting there for so long, sobbing. I don't care if she's the president. Pregnancy is a deeply humbling, mortifying experience. And coming from me, that's saying a lot.

Chapter 9

Princess Nicole

———∽◊◊∽———

The best part of pregnancy? Everyone—but everyone—acts like your shit doesn't stink, despite so much evidence to the contrary (see previous chapter). Pregnancy cast a magical spell on me. Poof! I was transformed into a friggin' princess.

Now, you might think I already got a lot of special treatment as a well-known person. I definitely have my fans (love you all, Boo Boos!). But by and large, when I am recognized on the street or in the airport, people don't say, "Hey, it's Snooki. Let's be really nice to her!" I wish! Mainly, people laugh at me, stare, or make fun of me to my face, calling me a troll and worse.

On the boardwalk in Seaside, people would randomly shout out "whore" and "retard" at me when all I was doing was throwing a dart at the balloon game or mixing a drink at the Make Your Own Slurpee stand. *Jersey Shore* fame didn't cast me in the most flattering, brightest light. More like a flashlight on the bottom of a Dumpster.

Getting arrested, doing shots, and hooking up with guys I just met in clubs earned me a certain reputation. Generally speaking, strangers didn't lift a finger for me, especially if I were falling down in the gutter. The one time I inspired gallantry on *Jersey Shore*, I had to get punched in the face first.

But being pregnant was a completely different story. People were sweet. They were happy to see me. I was a symbol of love and commitment that they could respect and admire. I guess a pregnant lady's distinctive shape touches off some ancient survival instinct in people's lizard brain. If the Neanderthals didn't take good care of their knocked up cavewomen, the species would die out. Dinosaurs would have replaced humans. Or whatever. Most people react lovingly and protectively—aka, the royal treatment—when they see you walking around with the Buddha belly.

When I entered a room, people stood up. It didn't matter where I was. Could be at home, at a restaurant, a waiting room, anywhere. I'd drag in my hugeness, and five people jumped out of their chairs like they were sitting on hot coals. I tested it. I'd walk by a bus shelter, even if I wasn't going to take the bus. The sight of a pregnant lady standing upright on two legs caused everyone on the bench to spring up and say, "Would you like a seat?" I was all too happy to accept the kind offers!

By month nine, just standing up was like running a marathon.

People made way for me. You know, like the trumpets blaring and the heralds shouting, "Make way for her royal highness!" I didn't have to announce my presence, though. I was so big, you'd have to be blind not to see me coming. People did have to get out of my way on the sidewalk or get knocked over. When I approached any door, someone would open it for me. If I were in a car, someone would offer me a hand to get in and out of it. When I went into a store to buy a snack, people would insist that I cut the line to pay. I loved it.

I didn't have to lift a finger. If I wanted to rest and put my feet up in the middle of the day, my friends and family would ask, "Can I get you a pillow?" They might be cooking or cleaning, but they never asked me to pitch in. I'm always willing to do my fair share around the house (not that I'm very good at it). But for the entire pregnancy, I got a hall pass on housework.

People served me. I didn't ask for this! But food just flowed my way. Jionni brought me meals to make sure I was eating all the right things. My mother-in-law-to-be brought me ice cream to improve my attitude. If I said, just to myself, or into the air, "I'm thirsty," a bottle of water would appear. A pregnant woman will never go thirsty or hungry. People were primed and eager to bring me stuff to eat, or to clear away the plates when I was done.

People bent over backwards to amuse me. My friends and family turned into court jesters, juggling and doing tricks for my entertainment. I wasn't a happy, smiley pregnant woman. My roomies and friends would tell me dirty jokes or do funny dance moves to crack me up. I will be forever grateful to everyone who made me laugh during that time. It was so needed and appreciated.

People flattered me nonstop. Everyone told me I was beautiful when I knew they were lying their asses off. It was like the law of the realm to tell the Pregnant Princess that she was radiant and glowing, when she really looked like doo that'd been dragged through a swamp. Jionni was a BOSS, telling me a hundred times a day that I was pretty and sexy. It's not vanity to need to hear that the father of your baby still thinks you're hot. When you're giant and miserable, getting a compliment might be the only thing that can get you up out of bed.

Insult me, and live to regret it. During the filming of *Jersey Shore* season six, Vinnie and I were rolling down the boardwalk on motorized scooters like a pair of oldies. We rode by the Aztec, and some jerkoff shouted, "Snooki, you fat whore" or "fat bitch." I wasn't sure. Anyway, Vinnie jumped off his scooter and went after the guy. "You call a pregnant women fat? What's wrong with you?" he yelled.

I'm sure Jionni would have torn the guy's head off, like a knight defending my honor. I'm not saying people haven't defended me before. But there was an intensity to the protectiveness when I was pregnant.

I could say whatever I wanted, and no one could go against me. By the seventh month, I realized I could get away with murder. So I would cause a scene and make people bring me food while Jionni massaged my feet. You can literally scream at your man, punch your friend, and break plates at the china store. Pregnancy gives you a pass to be a bitch.

As long as your belly shows, you will get sympathy. People will cater to your every whim. I definitely took advantage of the situation and I'm telling you to do the same! Don't feel bad about taking advantage. Pregnant Princess isn't a title you hold for long. As soon as you give birth, you abdicate the throne. So enjoy it while it lasts, ladies. Once your baby is out, being spoiled stops. I would die for Jionni to rub my feet and let me yell at him after being up for five hours in the middle of the night taking care of Lorenzo. But now I'm just a mom. Moms don't get the royal treatment. All the attention goes to the baby. As it should be! Lorenzo is definitely my little Prince.

Chapter 10

Butt Paste and Boogie Wipes

———◦◊◦———

For my baby shower, I needed a registry. I was psyched to go to Babies "R" Us to set it up. Who wouldn't be excited to pick through racks of onesies and footsie pajamas? I mean, the tiny sneakers alone . . . so freakin' cute. I thought I'd sign up for some clothes and cribbing to make gifting hassle-free for our friends and family. I had a vague sense that babies required a lot of stuff. Obviously, we had to have a crib, car seat, and stroller. But beyond that? A few fluffy towels, some soft toys and bottles. I had no idea what I was getting myself into. As soon as I walked into the store—which was bigger than an airplane hanger—I realized bedding and bottles were the least of it.

My mom and I went up to the desk and talked to a saleswoman about the process. They give you a scanner gun and you just walk around the place zapping the bar code of everything you want to put on your registry. Then your guests can log on to the website, see the items, check the ones they want to buy, and have them shipped right to your house already wrapped. That was all super easy. A chimp could use this system. What freaked me out were the *five million different things* you had to get—and the five million brands of each item to choose from.

The salesgirl started us in the breast section. I knew I was going to breastfeed because that was healthiest for my child. I thought it was pretty basic. You put the baby on your chest, and done. Wrong! I needed fifteen contraptions to do it. The pumps looked like medieval torture devices. The salesgirl demonstrated how it worked. It was *loud*. The suction was hard. I'm just like, "That's going to pull on my nipple? Is it going to get sucked off?" What the fuck was I getting myself into here?

I narrowed it down to a freestanding piston pump or a portable vacuum pump built into a backpack. The price difference was only like a hundred dollars. I went for the backpack pump, thinking, *It's only a hundred bucks more.* Along with the pump, I had to choose steam-cleaner bags, milk removal soap, pump wipes, replacement parts like membranes, valves, a "breast shield," custom-fit "flanges" (the funnel part you put against the boob), milk storage bottles, freezer bags, and a special breast milk feeding nipple to screw on the special breast milk feeding bottles.

Then we moved on to personal care breast products, like "nursing butter," a balm to smear on your nipples to prevent cracking. My nipples were *going to crack?* What the fuck?

If the butter didn't work, I needed nipple guards, either soft shell or hard plastic, or soothing gel pads to slap on my aching faucets. I also needed "bust cream," for skin softness, "firming butter," to make sagging boobs snap back, and "tummy butter," which comes in "belly brazil nut" or "cocoa butter," to rub on my belly and boobs to fix stretch marks. All this talk about cream, nuts, and butter, and I hadn't had lunch yet! Bwrahh, hungry! "Baby Kisses" lip balm would make Lorenzo's lips soft before he clamped down and sucked my mammaries inside out.

Of course, I had to get a supply of nipple pads to prevent that awkward moment when you were ordering the sushi platter and your milk gushed onto the floor. The pads came in disposable or washable, in circle or heart shaped, in five different colors, sizes, and strengths. I'd probably need the Maxi Nipple Pads. I could also choose from fifteen different nursing bras, for sleeping and/or bustier style for hands-free pumping. The bustier had holes in the middle of the cup, and not the sexy kind you see in sex shops. Nothing sexy in the entire store, by the way. I picked a nursing pillow (crescent? circle? wedge?), a nursing shawl, and a nursing poncho to cover the baby's snack time from the eyes of perverts. The Milkscreen home test for alcohol in breast milk was a must. That did come in handy later on, actually.

Still with me? And that was just the *first aisle*. I'd been there for fifteen minutes and my mind—already foggy from pregnancy—was reeling. All things boob total: $650.

After that, we registered for baby grooming products, like a baby nail clipper. A friend of mine told me she used to trim her baby's nails by biting them off. And when her baby got a cold, she put her mouth over his nose and literally sucked the snot out of it. That might be too gross even for me. I had to choose between a suction bulb or a battery operated nasal clear system that did the sucking for you, plus "Boogie Wipes" to clean up his snotty face. Other products to choose from: ear thermometers, humidifiers in the shapes of elephants and pigs, pacifiers, pacifier clips and storage pods, baby hairbrush, toothbrush, toothpaste, gum massager, baby wash and shampoo, bibs. Babies needed a lot rags for sopping up drool and puke. It'd be like Sunday morning at the shore house.

Moving to the ass section, they sold dozens of types, colors, and sizes of diapers, diaper covers, creams, and ointments. There was a product called "Butt Paste." Yum. Also ass wipes—large, small, organic, flushable, with aloe, scented, unscented. I could choose different caddies, aka a "Diaper Depot," to attach to the changing table with compartments for wipes, diapers, creams, and lotions, as well as nylon or plastic wipe travel pouches. I scanned the electric wipe warmer in a heartbeat. I wanted warm wipes for my own butt. Life changer!

Moms in the know didn't just throw dirty diapers in the garbage. I would need a special diaper cannon thingie. You could get a mechanical one that vacuum sealed each dirty diaper in odor-free plastic wrap. With the name Diaper Genie, it should be able to make diapers disappear. A cheaper choice was manual diaper baggies with twist ties (like people use for dog shit) that you tossed into a deodorized waste basket. I thought, *I'll get the one that's a little more expensive. What's another $40?* I passed on the "Wee Block." It's a little terry-cloth cup you put over the baby's penis when changing his diaper. I didn't mind the idea of Lorenzo peeing in my face, as long as it didn't get in my mouth.

Snot, drool, piss, and shit total: $600.

In the same aisle that sold baby utensils and bowls, food grinders, and food processors, you could also get a baby scale. Not to weigh his food. But to weigh the baby himself, to see if he was getting enough of all the goodies you put in the bowls and fed to him via spork. Speaking of goodies, there were hundreds of kinds of baby food and formula, in boxes, cups, squeeze packs, pouches, and jars. Not to mention the millions of bottles, nipples, electric bottle warmers, and bottle drying racks available. The weirdest product on that aisle was a mesh fruit sucker. You put a piece of fresh fruit into a mesh pouch. He'd suck the fruit through the mesh to avoid choking. A baby didn't just chill on the carpet while eating. He would sit in a high chair, or a low chair, or a floor seat, or a chair that is attached to the table. I scanned one of each. Total for all food and dining items: $700.

Seeing the trend? I was running up hundreds of dollars *per aisle*. Have I mentioned the baby-proofing section? Every item you could ever want to make your home safe, from gates to knob covers to cabinet locks. Plus, you could choose from a selection of "movement monitors" in audio and/or video. I liked the pretty cloud-shaped monitor but it was pricier than the others. I said in what became the registry's slogan, "What's another $50?"

My mom mentioned a few times that back when I was a baby, she didn't use most of this stuff. But then again, I was adopted at six months. The entire boob area didn't apply to her. And she didn't need the infant stuff, like the "Snuggle Nest," which was like a mini-bassinette with side rails to put in your bed to make sure you don't roll over and smother the kid. Another suffocation prevention product: the crib wedge. Back in the day, people just rolled up a blanket and put it next to a baby to keep him in a safe position on his back and prevent the five-alarm mayhem of his rolling onto his belly. But I read the wedge's packaging: "For your peace of mind." Well, wasn't my peace of mind worth $30?

Over in the bathing area, I had to laugh when I saw the $70 baby bubbling spa shower. It was a freestanding pink plastic hot tub that had a battery powered whirlpool machine attached to it! Baby Jacuzzi! Can I get in? If that was a little over the top, you could always get a smaller, less high-tech baby bather, along with a spout protector, and the bath stool for mommy to sit on next to the bathtub. My mom said she used to just put me in the kitchen sink to bathe me. When I got older, I went in the regular bathtub and she kneeled on the bathroom floor.

I didn't get anything in the potty training aisle. It would be a while before Lorenzo used a plastic toilet. I did check out the "Potty wrist watch" that beeps an "It's time to go!" alarm. We'd been there an hour already. I had to run to the Babies "R" Us bathroom every twenty minutes. I didn't need an alert to tell me to pee. I have never, to my recollection, needed help figuring out when I had to relieve myself. If Lorenzo was anything like his mom, he wouldn't either. When nature calls, my boy will answer on the first ring!

So far, I'd registered for a hundred little things and already spent thousands. We hadn't even gotten to the big-ticket items yet. If I thought I had a rough time deciding between nipple creams, I had no idea how hard it would be to choose a stroller. Which was the safest, the best, the coolest? I definitely needed an infant stroller with a detachable car seat/carrier. But I'd also need a stroller for when he was older. What about an "all-terrain" stroller? Was I going to be a mom who jogs around the neighborhood? Uh, no. My milk would cascade out of my boobs from bouncing.

A stroller was not complete without accessories, such as a phone holder, a cup holder, a "toy bar" (not nearly as fun as it sounds), food trays, a canopy, baskets, and a fan or umbrella. I tried to picture myself lifting up a tricked-out stroller to go up the steps. Could I do it? The lightest stroller was only sixteen pounds with a titanium frame, and it cost (brace yourself) $500. I was tempted, but I couldn't pull that trigger. For a while, we'd carry Lorenzo in a Baby Bjorn, or a sling, or a Snugglie, or a baby backpack—with a frame or without. By now, my brain had melted all over the floor. Clean up in the stroller aisle! Get the mop.

Car seats were another necessity that you had to upgrade every twenty pounds—infant rear facing, baby front facing, then a booster seat—with all the accessories, including a Snuzzler head rest to protect his neck, which, considering my driving, was essential. Of course, we needed the portable crib for $300. Unfolded, it was a full size playpen with changing table. Folded, it was the size of a Tampon box. I'd heard from other moms that a bouncy seat and a baby swing were must-haves. One of the swings rocked, vibrated, and swayed at five speeds and included a toy bar, plush cushions, an LED light show, and an MP3 player. It wasn't a baby seat, it was a disco party cruise! If they made one for grownups, I'd never get out of it. Only $250!

And then there were the *real* necessities that will keep your baby from screaming in your ear. As I came to learn, the best choice was a $2 pacifier. I registered for a few of those, along with play gyms, activity centers, a million toys, and security blankets. I nearly added an entire Hello, Kitty! furniture set that included a zebra patterned armchair. It looked like the high heel chair I have for myself. A lot of the kid furniture looked like my stuff. Hmmm. It made me wonder ... but not too much.

So the grand total of everything I scanned and added to my registry was . . . wait for it . . . $5,400! According to the sales girl, that was around average. My little guy wasn't even there yet, and he was costing a lot of pesos! It would be thousands to feed, transport, entertain, comfort, and clean the crap off a six-pound critter—and that was only for the first few months of his life. By comparison, a six-pound cat costs about $200 *a year*. But obviously, a baby is not a human pet. No fur.

No one *needed* a baby Jacuzzi or baby disco cruise. But I registered for all of it anyway. I didn't know what I was doing as a mom, but if I had all the stuff, and it was all new and modern, it might make motherhood easier. I hated the idea of being in a situation where, say, a butt paste would really come in handy, and I didn't have it. I'm sure the makers and sellers of baby products are aware that they play to a new mom's fears. Every time I scanned a barcode, I knew I was being suckered. But I didn't care.

I've been told that feeling overwhelmed while registering—and the reality of what you were getting yourself into—is a rite of passage for first-time moms. "With your second baby, you won't use 90 percent of this stuff," women have said. We actually needed a van to transport it all to the house from the baby shower. The spare bedroom was packed floor to ceiling. Though a lot of it never got used, I did take some comfort in knowing it was all there.

Of all that stuff, the **Must Haves** would have to be ...

The baby bouncy seat.

The baby swing.

The diaper caddy (it does keep things organized).

The bottle warmer (since I was freezing so much milk).

The item that really worked to entertain and calm Lorenzo didn't come from the baby store. It came from the Apple Store. Lorenzo loves his iPad. We have it strapped to his crib. He's not even a year old and he knows how to get to his favorites tunes and videos. Some people might criticize us for letting a baby play with an electronic device. If you don't know by now, I don't care what my critics say. Let my baby live! He loves his music and rocks out in his crib every night. He is part of the first generation born with devices in their hands, and good on him. We plan to use the iPad to teach him to read and do math. He's going to be a pro with it when he starts school, and that's only positive.

Most Useful Item: nipple cream. When I first saw it on the shelf, I thought I was in the wrong store. Were we in Babies "R" Us, or the

Pleasure Chest? Nipple cream would be more at home among dildos than diapers, or so I thought. Um, I was completely wrong. This nipple cream isn't to get you off or in the mood. It saved my nipples from falling off. After pumping, my poor pepperonis were ON FIRE! Putting the cream on made them feel like popsicles in the freezer—so relieving. New moms should buy nipple cream by the quart. You will use it, and rely on it, heavily.

And the **Don't Bother Withs . . .**

All the sporks and special bowls. Just use regular stuff. The baby doesn't care what utensil you use.

The stroller attachments. They block the baby's view. Lorenzo is curious. He wants to see the world, not stare at a plastic flower.

The baby bath. Just like Mom said, the kitchen sink is easier.

Most Useless Items: super cute clothes. Registering for too many cute outfits is a common first baby mistake. We signed up for a closet full of stuff. Whoops. Lorenzo never wore half of it. We had this vision of him crawling around in cute button downs, trousers with snaps, and ties. (If he were a girl, it would have been tutus and crowns.) But those special outfit days hardly ever happened. It was all about the white onesies, bibs, and pajamas. I guess we could have put him in

Sunday clothes every day. But babies are a freakin' mess. One spit up, and their precious outfits are ruined. Now all those shirts and ties are in storage, waiting for the next baby boy who will probably never wear them.

Chapter 11

Bump vs. Blimp

———— ⚬⚬⚬ ————

You could have the healthiest body image in the world and still struggle with what happens to you during pregnancy. Anyone who's had an eating disorder or an obsession with size is going to have a really rough time of it.

My history with my body image has been shaky. My low point was back in high school. I was a cheerleader. I absolutely lived for it, and practiced for hours each day. I was the "flyer," the girl who got thrown around and stood at the top of the pyramid. I choreographed a lot of our routines and always put in some crazy dramatic throws that had me soaring through the air. I loved it. Cheering was my passion.

When I was a senior, I should have been enjoying my last year as a veteran on the team. But I saw all these new, tiny, fourteen-year-old freshman girls coming up through the ranks. They looked like babies. Not only were they skinny—like 89 pounds—they were small all over, flexible and fearless. Some of them were openly vying for my spot as flyer. I felt threatened by them. As petite as I was, these girls were even smaller.

Give up my place at the top of the pyramid? That was not going to happen. I added hours of practice to my day. I killed myself staying in shape. I was determined to make myself as tiny as the freshman girls. So I cut way back on food. I went from normal eating to just having salads and a handful of crackers each day. Then just one salad and one cracker. Then just one cracker. It got to the point that I ate only ice cubes, all day, for days in a row.

I didn't stop eating to look hot, or to be the prettiest girl at school, or because I had a messed-up childhood. No deep-seated emotional or psychological problems or insecurities to report. Sorry. I wasn't trying to starve myself into looking like models in magazines or actresses in the movies. I was motivated only by the fear of losing my spot as flyer. I was competing with younger, lighter girls, and thought this was the way to win. The irony was, I was so hungry and tired from not eating, I almost fainted during practice. I managed to starve myself until I was smaller than the freshman girls. But I wasn't healthy or strong. What good was a skinny flyer if she passed out from hunger and fell off the pyramid?

I sort of knew that I wasn't really helping myself by whittling my body down to tan and bone. But I was in the anorexia zone. As weak and tired as it made me, starvation was self-destructively addicting. I felt a sense of accomplishment for getting through a day on water and air. That pride doubled if I could do it the next day, too. The rational side of me knew this wasn't a good idea. I wanted to start eating again, but it was like I forgot how to do it. I was afraid of what would happen if I did. I thought I'd gain twenty pounds overnight, that all my self-denial would be erased by one cheeseburger.

The year was 2006. My bout with anorexia was decades after *The Best Little Girl in the World.* The disease was way out there in the media and had been for a long time. We'd done a whole course on eating disorders in junior high health class and were constantly reminded about it in magazines and on TV. Despite the fact that everyone seemed to know about anorexia, including me, I managed to fly under the radar for a few months without anyone noticing how skinny I was getting. I think they just thought of me as small to begin with.

The school nurse was the first person to clue in. I went into her office to weigh myself every day. I didn't do it on the down low, like creeping into the room when she wasn't looking. I just went in, stepped on the scale, and left. A lot of girls did the same thing. But this was an observant lady. She not only noticed that I weighed myself, but that the number was going down, from 105, to 100, to 90, and eventually, down to a seriously fucked-up low of 80 pounds. Forget the freshman girls. My weight was lower than a sixth grader's.

The nurse called my parents. "Get Nicole to a doctor," she told Mom. "Her weight is too low. She's not eating. Something's wrong with her." I'm not sure if the nurse raised the eating disorder flag, or she just let my parents assume. When someone loses weight that fast, it could be any number of things. I actually had to get some tests to prove to my parents that it wasn't that I was sick with a medical disease. I was making myself sick.

I don't know exactly how I managed to break out of that "must not eat" mindset. Just calling attention to it, my parents watching me like a hawk, and my friends catching on and supporting me combined to loosen the grip of it. When cheerleading ended for the season, I just started eating again, adding foods and meals pretty quickly. It was almost like I was making up for lost time. I got back up to my normal weight by graduation.

Being obsessed with weight—for whatever reason—only caused trouble. I wanted to look good. But even more than that, I wanted to have fun. College was all about studying hard, and partying harder. I traded hours of cheerleading workouts for hours knocking back beers and shots. The pounds really piled on.

When I auditioned for *Jersey Shore* at age twenty, I weighed 110 pounds. The GTL lifestyle, for me, wasn't exactly slimming. I usually skipped the "G" part of it and never hit the gym. I hit the bar. The only exercise I got those first couple of years on the show was dancing and running from the police. If you watch seasons one and two of *Jersey Shore*, you can clearly see that I was getting chubbier episode by episode. I'd taken the "I'm happy with myself" attitude to the extreme. Honestly, I didn't care what anyone else said about me. People called me a "bowling ball" or a "basketball." Whatever. You gotta let the haters hate, or you'll go crazy. What they said had nothing to do with who I was as a person. My goal was to just be true to my natural shape and myself. I was born with a petite, curvy body. I loved food and partying. I'd rather have a blast than deny myself—or slide back into an eating disorder.

But, being true to yourself doesn't mean just letting it all go and not being healthy. Those first few years on the show, I took the art of not giving a shit as a far as a person could. I had fleeting moments of thinking, "I love myself no matter what, but this isn't my natural size. I'm naturally smaller." I tried dieting a few times, including an insane plan of eating only high protein cookies. That didn't last. One margarita later, I'd find myself elbow deep in a platter of nachos. I was in a heavy "Why deny myself?" mode that included a lot of Long Island iced teas and funnel cakes. Whatever I wanted was okay—which wasn't *really* okay, no matter how I justified it.

After some awards show, I looked at the photos of me on the red carpet and thought, *Okay, that's gone far enough*. Even if the camera added ten pounds, I was larger than I'd ever been at 126. Remember, I'm only 4'9". I'd put on twenty pounds since college, and it was all vodka and onion rings. I'd had enough of it. I thought, *Packing on flab is not loving myself*.

It was a real eye-opener. You can have good self-esteem and still groan over bad pictures. Just as it's okay to put on a few pounds, it's also okay to say to yourself, "Seriously, I need to get my house in order." I watched myself on TV, and I just didn't like what I saw. The press was showing old photos of me as a high school cheerleader and calling attention to how different I looked. I wanted to get back to that range. Not the anorexic 80 pounds, but a built and ripped 100 to 105 when my legs were rock solid muscle. Everyone who has had periods of her life when she was fit knows what it means to be strong and sexy. You just feel better all day, physically and mentally. I'd been eating junk for years. I had to put an end to it. I'd veered from one extreme to the other. The time had come to get in shape.

It took all of 2011 to do it. I busted my ass and got back down to my high school weight of 105. I lived at the gym, and ate a farm's worth of greens and grilled chicken. I drank booze only when filming. During the off-months, I just had vodka seltzers or a sip or two of wine. It's no coincidence that I got my body back in shape at the same time I was in a relationship with Jionni. I wanted to be sexy and lean for myself, but also for him. The best part of the change was that I didn't feel like a fat slob anymore. I looked in the mirror and thought, *Mmwah! I love that sexy bitch.* I got down to a size two and felt the right kind of pride. For the cover of my second novel, *Gorilla Beach*, I posed in a *very* tiny monokini and rocked it. I was in love with Jionni and with my chiseled body.

I was actually a week or two pregnant at that photo shoot and didn't know it. When we finally realized I'd missed my period for a reason, it was the start of a new year. No resolution to lose weight this time around! I had one lousy month at my goal weight, and then, almost as soon as I peed on those sticks, the fat layer came creeping back on. Being hot and sexy was what got me into this situation. That, and not using condoms. (Never again. My next pregnancy will be planned.) I was excited about having a baby and getting engaged to the love of my life. But I did have to wrap my mind around more body changes. I'd just spent a year losing twenty pounds. I barely got to enjoy being in sick shape, and now I was going to gain all of the weight back, plus another . . . who knows? I had no idea how huge I'd be by the end. AWESOME.

During the first trimester, I ate for five. The wild hunger dipped around month four. But did I scale back? No way! Food was my comfort when I felt otherwise miserable. I had to eat more for the baby's sake. My pregnancy apps said you only needed to increase your intake by 300 calories per day—the equivalent of a banana and some milk. I tried to stick to that and not give in to the-round-the-clock ice cream cravings. Three hundred calories got eaten up pretty fast. By the third trimester, my stomach was so squished by my growing uterus, I could only eat small amounts at a time. I still managed to down a lot of brownies. My number one food craving was for watermelon. I ate tons of it. Maybe that explained my gas pains.

I couldn't exercise. I could barely muster the energy to go up a flight of stairs. If a woman can work out her whole pregnancy, props to her. My ass stayed on the couch.

In the early months, I didn't look pregnant. I looked bloated like I went to Burger King for breakfast, lunch, and dinner every day. Before long, my body started doing alien, abnormal things. It wasn't recognizable to me. I got a line down my belly, and not from a bronzer accident. My nipples got as big as jellyfish, and turned dark. My boobs sagged like saddlebags. My face got round and puffy. I had zits all over my face and chest. Cellulite was a new thing for me. If I squeezed my leg, I could see cottage cheese. I hate cottage cheese.

When I started to show about month five, I was ecstatic to look pregnant. Finally, I had a bump! But by month six, I couldn't see my vagina anymore. That was when shit got real. Some parts got fat, and some just retained water like a ShamWow. For the first time in my life, I had cankles. My fingers were like Vienna sausages. I had always loved my slim legs and hands. My rings got so tight, I took most of them off. Not my engagement ring, though. That sucker is staying on, even if it cuts my finger off.

My body grew by the hour. I started missing the days when I just looked like a fat ass. I thought I couldn't possibly get any wider. And then I did, again and again. My belly button turned inside out. By the end of my pregnancy, I was as big around as I am tall. At a certain point, I stopped looking in the mirror naked. The fat and bloat weren't here to stay. I knew that. But I still didn't like to see it. I threw on my blouses and oversize t-shirts in bright colors, flat ironed my hair, put on makeup, and hoped I looked okay.

I made the rookie mistake of trying to hide all of my emotions about this issue during the filming of *Snooki & JWOWW* and *Jersey Shore*. Once or twice, I slipped and complained, because there was only so much I could take. I tried to button my lips about feeling fat. I didn't want to seem like a needy pregnant bitch, or to be obsessed about my weight. But after a time, I realized, *Hello! I AM a pregnant, needy bitch*. People could plainly see that I was a blimp. Not complaining about the most obvious, horrible symptom of the experience—transforming into a whale before everyone's eyes—would have been weird and wrong. It was a fact of creating life. I couldn't hide my emotions any more than my belly.

So much is made in the media about celebrity pregnancy weight gain. Some women have been mocked cruelly for it. Tabloid monitoring of how fast women lose the baby weight is practically a blood sport. If you weren't on the cover of *In Touch* in a bikini within two months of giving birth to talk about your salsa workout, you were a fat, lazy loser. Just look at how Jessica Simpson and Kim Kardashian were tracked and criticized in the media. Awful! Worrying about weight gain made the nine months even harder. The one bright spot of pregnancy was eating whatever you wanted. Being afraid or depressed about getting fat—and criticized for it—destroyed even that joy.

Like whales traveling in a pod, I really liked hanging with other pregnant ladies. We understood each other. We were our own species. When I returned to the skinny, partying, drinking chicks in bandage dresses, I felt pissed off. Jealousy of other women only hit hard when Jionni noticed them.

Warning: Do not watch movies with your man that feature young, hot, , non-pregnant girls who show their boobs and ass. One movie night we decided to watch *Piranha*. Worst decision ever. It turned out to be 90 minutes of skinny girls in bikinis on Spring Break, drinking, making out, and getting eaten by killer fish. I stared at Jionni, checking for the faintest sign he was into them. "Stop looking at me. I'm just watching the movie!" he said with his tongue practically hanging out. The last thing I need was to see my man mesmerized by hot bitches while I was sitting right next to him, enormous on the sofa. I thought, *Kill me now*. Or, better, *Kill him*. So my pregnant psycho ass started screaming, "GO BE WITH THEM THEN!" That escalated into a huge fight. He slept on the couch while I cried myself to sleep. I thought I'd never look skinny and sexy again. Welp, WRONGO. I got my body back. Eat that, *Piranha* bitches.

It still isn't safe to go back into the water. After that night, we avoided that particular aggravation and watched *The Three Stooges* and other movies starring fat old men.

It wasn't until late in the pregnancy that I fully accepted what was happening. I just let it sink in that there was no other choice. The last thing a pregnant woman needs to stress about is weight. She should just eat healthy and try to remain calm and comfortable. She has every right to enjoy eating what she loves and taking a mental break from the battle to be slim. It got a lot better for me when I let all that go. It was like flicking a switch and deciding not to freak out. I was lending my body to my baby for several months. When it was over, I'd lose the weight. I'd done it before, and I would do it again. Until then, I'd enjoy the brownies. If Jionni offered to make me a grilled cheese sandwich and slice up a watermelon for me, I let him. In fact, the only time I didn't cry or yell at him was when he brought me food.

In all, I gained 44 pounds. Not a lot for a regular size woman, but I was 105 pounds to start. I'd put on about 40 percent of my overall body weight. Proportionally, if I'd weighed 150 to start and gained 40 percent, I would have been 210 at the end. In those last weeks, I was so beyond giving a shit about my weight. I was gaining a child. Who cared about pounds?

I was so at ease with my shape, Jionni and I made a plaster cast of my belly and boobs. He wet the plaster strips and smoothed them over my body. I had to wait forever for it to dry. And then, it was a memento of just how ginormous I was. I tried it on the other day, five months postpartum. It was like a whole other person was on top of me. We're going to save it and break it out of the attic one day when Lorenzo is sixteen. I can see it now. He'll invite his girlfriend over, and I'll say, "Wanna see the cast of my boobs when I was pregnant with Lorenzo?"

He'll be so embarrassed! Hehe.

Chapter 12

Super Mommy

E very pregnant lady is a superhero for what she goes through. She's brave and courageous, with incredible strength to haul her belly around. With great pregnancy comes great responsibility— and great powers. I definitely gained some Super Mommy skills. (Transforming into a Hindenburg was not one of them. That was not super.)

For the most part, having preggers powers was pretty cool. The only one I was not into was . . .

Super Smell. It was like I was bitten by a radioactive basset hound. I could sniff out a French fry within ten miles, and zero in on it like a blip on a radar screen. French fry, dead ahead! I knew if Jionni sneaked upstairs for a shot, which he did sometimes for stress relief, as soon as he uncapped the bottle. The smell of vodka on him was so strong, it was like he took a bath in it. If I was within two hundred feet of a garbage can, I could smell it and detected what was inside—coffee grinds, check, eggshells, check, used condoms, ECCCH! And then I could visualize myself gagging into it. Even normal, nice scents like the ocean or suntan lotion that I'd otherwise enjoy became overpowering. The whole world reeked! I have no idea how dogs can get through their lives like this. A pregnant dog? How does she *survive*? Super smell for me was just disgusting. I warded off the grossness by dabbing Snooki perfume under my nostrils throughout the day.

Okay, on to the super powers I loved.

Super Balance. I'm going to reveal my secret power source during my pregnancy: my Jeffrey Campbells. I got a lot of shit for wearing heels. Critics said that the so-called ankle-breakers were dangerous because I might fall down and hurt the baby. But unless I fell down a flight of stairs and ruptured the placenta, my tumbling the five feet from standing upright in heels to landing on my fat ass was not going to hurt the baby. The uterus muscles and amniotic fluid were like a baby bomb shelter, keeping him nice and safe in there. Plus, I've been living in heels since I was a teenager. I was steadier in six-inch heels than in flats. I guess I was living down a reputation for falling down drunk. But I wasn't drunk when pregnant. I was one thousand percent sober. And when I was sober, I was as stable as Mount Everest.

In fact, when my belly got big, my balance was even better. It was like Lorenzo was my inner stabilizer. A couple of times, I did teeter. It seemed like Lorenzo was there to catch me and keep me from falling. The one and only time I stumbled and had to take a knee during my entire nine months of pregnancy? I was wearing platform flats!

Super Dreams. Apparently, most preggers ladies have vivid dreams. It's due to hormones (bitches!) and having to wake up every five minutes to run to the bathroom holding your crotch. If you wake up in the middle of a dream, you remember the colors and details more clearly. When I was two months along and had only just found out, I dreamed I was nine months pregnant and hadn't gained any weight. Texting Dr. Freud! Some dreams *are* wish fulfillment. Jionni and I were at the W Hotel in New York. My mom was there, too. She whipped out a huge syringe and injected me to induce labor. Instantly, I got terrible contractions. The pain woke me up. In real life, I wasn't having false labor or anything scary. It was gas. Thanks, ass.

My dreams got scarier as the pregnancy progressed. In one of my nightmares, I was on my phone in the jungle. Lions and tigers were sitting all around me. I adore all animals, especially felines. But these weren't cuddly, fluffy house cats. They were vicious monsters with teeth dripping blood and spit. They were also on their phones, tweeting with their claws that they were going to eat me. I read that dreaming of animals is common during the second trimester. But usually, they are bunnies and puppies, cute fur balls that represented the helplessness innocence of a little baby. How to interpret my dream about being fresh meat for savage beasts?

"The jungle could be your crazy life in public," Jionni said. "The lions and tigers are the pressures and fears that it might eat you alive."

"Or maybe I just fell asleep watching *Animal Planet,*" I said.

The classic third-trimester dream is about actually giving birth. It is the subconscious way of getting ready for what is to come. Your subconscious' shows you the trailer of your birth movie. My doctor told me that scary birth dreams are a way of mentally preparing for anything. Your sleeping mind is addressing all those fears that you might not be able to talk or think about when you are awake.

By that theory, I was really well prepared to give birth! I had a dream that I squeezed out a baby, but it wasn't Lorenzo. It was a Chucky doll. He came out of my vagina covered in blood. His doll head turned 360 degrees on a wooden neck, and he looked at me like he wanted to kill me. The nurses put him on my chest. He smiled with razor sharp teeth. I threw him off the bed, screaming in total panic. Then the Chucky newborn did a somersault in mid-air, landed on his feet, ran toward the bed, jumped back on my chest and went for my jugular. He might've scooped up the placenta along the way and gobbled that down, too. So creepy.

One more third-trimester dream: I was driving down the Garden State Parkway in my tricked out Range Rover (with the pinkwashed wheels and grill). I thought of it as my New Mommy Car, because it was as big and safe as a tank. I was doing eighty, enjoying the drive. Then the trunk popped open, and all the stuff in the back went flying out on the highway, including a hundred pairs of leopard print shoes, which got run over by the oncoming traffic.

"You're in the New Mommy Car, and all your old stuff gets tossed out the door," said Jionni about that one. "Pretty obvious, Nicole."

"A reminder to always double check the trunk?"

Just kidding! I knew what he meant. Leopard shoes represented the old me, the party girl. The car was my new life as a proud mama. There just wasn't room in my new life for all the old baggage. Whether I wanted to or not, I had to leave that stuff behind on the Garden State Parkway of Life. Well, not *everything*, I hoped. Moms can still rock leopard heels! I kept mine, and after a few weeks postpartum when I wasn't so swollen anymore, they fit my feet, and my new life, just fine.

Super Psychic Ability. I only got a few glimmers of mind-reading during my pregnancy. Each time, it was, honest to shit, the most amazing experience of the entire nine months. I read Lorenzo's mind. He talked to me with his brain waves. He told me what music he wanted to listen to, and what he wanted me to eat. He asked for watermelon a lot, so the kid had a real sweet tooth. I felt like we had silent conversations about how we couldn't wait to meet each other.

When he was born, and we looked each other in the eye, it was like I already knew him. Call me crazy, but it seemed like he recognized me, too.

Chapter 13

Does the Crib Come in Leopard Print?

~~~~~~~

When the final season of *Jersey Shore* wrapped, I returned to our apartment in Jionni's parents' basement. I was nearly eight months pregnant. Filming had been emotionally bumpy, especially at the end. We were all sad to say goodbye. It was truly the end of an era for MTV, and also for me personally. For one thing, I was no longer a professional fuck up. In just over a month, I would be a responsible mom.

I could finally start preparing for Lorenzo's arrival. I thought I could do it full time, but something came up. *Snooki & JWOWW* Season One aired while we were filming *Jersey Shore*. It was a hit. The producers decided to start shooting Season Two *right away*. One of the first days of shooting was at my baby shower. Most of the stuff I registered for came in, along with a ton of other gifts. (Thanks so much, everyone!) My fave was a motorcycle rocking horse and Gucci baby booties. The boxes and baby supplies were crammed into a spare bedroom at the house while we fixed up the basement.

It was an open space that we divided into different "rooms." In one corner, we put our bed. In the opposite corner, we intended to put Lorenzo's crib. It was currently occupied by a pool table. Another corner would be the living room with a couch and TV. The last was already a kitchenette with a table and chairs. Next to the kitchen was a bar. Now that I wasn't drinking, I was going to live ten feet from an open bar. Kewl. We'd have to move a lot of furniture down there, and clear out decades' worth of stored junk that had to be hauled up the stairs.

Not by me, duh. I was huge and pregnant.

Jionni and I went shopping for a crib at Bellini in Short Hills. The crib was super important. It would be where my baby would sleep. Sleep was a top three favorite activity of mine, and my bed was my little island. I took my bedding—duvet, pillows, and sheets—with me wherever I went. My son would probably (hopefully) be a good sleeper, too. To make sure of it, I wanted to get him the Cadillac of cribs.

We chose the Debby design with a mahogany finish, plus the Domani changing table, dresser, and armoire, also in mahogany. They were dark and masculine, and would match the hardwood floors. The design was classy. For a touch of gaudiness, I chose bling-bling rhinestone drawer pulls. We also ordered a cream-colored shag rug so Lorenzo would have a soft landing when he learned to crawl.

I had a bit of a snit at the store when the saleswoman said the name of one of the crib designs, "Jessica," and Jionni repeated it in a sexy voice. Like he had the hots for some girl named Jessica. He thought he was being funny. So not. It really pissed me off. Fortunately (for him), we were in a public place.

The pool table had to go to make room for the crib. Jionni dismantled it with a friend. I focused on setting up my bathroom and our "bedroom." Before I could tackle all the baby stuff, I had to get our parts of the apartment livable first. My urge to make a nice place for Lorenzo's arrival wasn't typical "nesting." We didn't live in a tree. We lived underground. We were "lairing," making a cozy, safe cave for our little family.

If Jionni approved, I would have done up Lorenzo's space in leopard print, ceiling to carpet. But he thought that was too girlie for a boy. Jionni loves sports. He really wanted Lorenzo to be an athletic kid like his daddy, so we did a very classic sports theme with balls on the walls (literally), along with huge stuffed animals for a jungle feel.

I got my animal print fix with a custom-designed leopard print baby blanket and crib bumper.

I started to feel physically horrible around this time (graphic details in the next chapter). The heartburn and gas were intense. I could barely stand up, let alone decorate. Until the crib and furniture arrived, there wasn't much else to do. Cameras were in position all over the house, filming me sitting around, moping, twiddling my thumbs, feeling like crap.

If only I could've done more. Getting everything in order is how soon-to-be moms distract themselves toward the end. During my downtime without stuff to do, I started thinking about the fact that soon, I was going to push a bowling ball out of my vagina. At the last sonogram, we learned Lorenzo was already six pounds. I still had four weeks to go.

I was torn between fear of giving birth and a desperate longing to meet my baby. The sonogram images blew my mind. I could see myself in his face. Not only was Lorenzo my first child, but he was also my first blood relative. I mean, the first blood relative I would actually know. I was adopted in Chile when I was six months old. My parents Andy and Helen have been awesome parents, just beyond loving and caring. They are so great, I've never really cared what happened back in Chile, who my bio parents are, and why they gave me up. I have asked Mom if she knows anything about them, but she has always changed the subject. I don't push. It obviously upsets her. I know some adopted kids feel a hole in their soul that only info about their birth parents can fill. Not me. The first six months of my life might be an interesting story. I just don't need or want to know it.

When we found out about the pregnancy, though, Jionni brought up the subject of my adoption. He wanted to know more details about my bio parents' health history. Mom said, "They were healthy." She didn't offer more. I asked Jionni not to bring it up again. He'd have to be satisfied to know they were healthy, and obviously *very sexy*. What more did he need? And what would he do with more information, if he had it? What if Mom told him my birth parents had a family history of heart disease or leprosy? He wasn't going to reject the baby or me. Lorenzo would be strong and healthy because Jionni and I took care of ourselves, and we would take care of him. He'd have the best medical care in the world, plus loving parents and grandparents. No worries! I definitely hoped Lorenzo looked a bit like me. But I really hoped he'd look like my hottie hubbie. Chances were, he would. Jionni has some seriously strong genes. He and his relatives all look alike. And there are so many of them!

During that final month, I got a crash course in diaper changing on my newborn nephew-to-be. It was kind of a disaster. I couldn't stand the smell of shit. The fact that I had to wipe it and smear it around made me gag. My hope was that, when it was my own kid's shit, it would be different.

That was the kind of getting my house in order that would prepare me the most. The crib delivery really wasn't as important as the idea—really, the hope and faith—that I'd be okay with my baby's shit. That I could change the diapers I'd set up in such neat stacks. Becoming a mother was bigger than furniture arrangement and decorating. More than the right set up, I needed the right mindset. I psyched myself up, saying out loud, "I'm going to be a good mom." I kept saying it over and over. Not that I convinced myself. I was nervous and borderline freaked out. But I think I convinced Lorenzo. When a pregnant lady talked to herself, someone else was also listening.

Chapter 14

The Oldest 24-Year-Old in History

———

I woke up one morning and moaned, "Oh, my aching back!" Then I limped on my sore legs and feet over to the bathroom. Constipation, of course. My strength was sapped. I could barely crawl back to bed before I fell over from exhaustion.

Was I 24, or 84? I was creaking around like an oldie. That glowing pregnant lady whose skin is dewy and fresh and looks transcendently radiant as she glides through the day, bursting with energy and joy? She. Does. Not. Exist. Making a baby sucks out your beauty, energy, and youth. Don't worry. You get it all back. But in the meantime, embrace being temporarily elderly. During my last trimester, I aged 100 years in three months, and turned into a crotchety, perpetually pissed off crone who cornered you to tell you about her horrible, agonizing aches and pains. SUCH AS:

Hot flashes. Not just for menopause! They strike pregnant ladies, too. I was overheated anyway; the summer of 2012 was on fire with a month straight of 100 degree days. On top of that suffocating heat, I got hormonal hot flashes. It felt like a wildfire rampaging across my face and chest. I turned into the Human (Whale) Torch. Sweat poured down my face and between my cantaloupe boobs. And all of this yumminess was caught on camera. Whenever I felt a hot flash coming on, I wanted to strip and get straight into a cold shower.

Lower back pain. I walked hunched over from soreness like I'd gone crazy with the kettlebell at the gym. I decided that meant pregnancy was like a workout, and that my back and arm muscles were getting in great shape despite not lifting a feather for months. Look, when you're pregnant, you grasp at any straw.

General weakness. I was never like Ronnie with bulging muscles, but I did tone up before the pregnancy. Then I stopped working out, and started sleeping twelve hours a day. All my muscles disappeared. I felt feeble. I struggled to lift the TV remote. I could barely push the buttons. I swear. I had to grunt like a tennis player to change the channel. I dragged myself around the house. Jionni had to push me up and down those freakin' stairs. The only thing that gave me a little energy boost was dancing. I put on some tunes and let it all go, the stress, the weariness, the pain. The baby loved it. He'd dance inside while I frolicked around the room. I ran out of breath quickly, though. I lasted about five minutes before I had to take a seat. Then I'd snap my fingers and dance like a senior citizen on the couch. Cricket city.

Swollen feet. My feet were puffed up like pickled pig trotters. Horrible. Every step made my skin stretch almost to splitting. At around eight months, I had to give up my heels and switch to flip flops and slippers.

Sciatica. Classic old lady move, putting a hand on her hip and whining, "My sciatica!" Yeah, that was me. I started to get shooting pain in my left upper butt cheek. It was nerve compression due to my shifting uterus and pelvis. I couldn't stand up for longer than an hour. Sometimes, to take some of the pressure off my hips, I got on my hands and knees and crawled. Holy all fours! I felt like a cow with full udders hanging down. Sexy.

Saggy boobs. They went from hurting to aching to porn star enormous to drooping down to my navel from sheer heft. My areolas spread across my boob like pancake batter in a pan. They darkened, too. Picture it: My huge saddle bag tits with the giant brown nipples pointing at my swollen feet. Can you believe Jionni still wanted to have anything to do with me? Even like this, I had to fight him off.

Stretch marks. I tried to prevent them by exfoliating after the shower. Every morning, I rubbed my belly and boobs with moisturizer, like polishing honeydews. I hoped my skin wouldn't stretch but it did, around the eighth month. I got ugly lines around my belly and boobs. When the skin snapped back after the birth, they stayed red. Oh, well. I wouldn't cry about it. Stretch marks were like badges of honor. I'd been through a lot to get them. I earned my tiger strips. Rawr!

Bulge. I had a baby belly, not a beer belly. But they had the same feel. You know that hard, round, fat gut guys get after a lifetime of Budweiser and Doritos? The "I haven't seen my dick since disco" look? Yeah, my belly was like that. It took on frightening dimensions. It entered the room five minutes before I did. Only a few months earlier, I was so excited when I stopped looking like a bagel addict and started looking like like a real preggers lady. How could I have ever wanted my belly to grow (and grow, and grow)? Every pregnant women makes an *Alien* joke at some point, like she's about to split open and a hungry creature would emerge, teeth first, from her belly. I felt like it could happen any second, and that it'd be a relief.

Splotchy skin. My skin got progressively worse, and was really bad toward the end. Along with zits all over my chest, I finally got the dreaded facial mask. My skin got dark splotches on the cheeks and chin. It's caused by increased production of melanin, the same pigment stuff that gives color to freckles and hair. It even makes you tan. I was feeling pretty pleased with myself about not getting the mask—until I did. Guess I deserved it for being smug. Apparently, the darker your skin is naturally, the more likely you are to get splotches. If only I could have evened it out with bronzer. I didn't dare try. I might've only made it worse. I used foundation for damage control.

The shits. After nine months of constipation, my bowels finally loosened up at the end. That was actually a good thing, except I still had to spend hours in the bathroom. My poops got friggin' *enormous*. I never knew something so big could come out of me. As shocked as I was, I was proud, too. If I could push out a dinosaur poop, surely I could give birth.

Sleep trouble. You know how old people say they need only four hours of sleep a night? I needed a lot more, but four hours was pretty much what I got. At eight months, I couldn't get comfortable, even in the fetal position. I'd lie down and imagine Lorenzo also in the fetal position. I hoped he wasn't as frustrated as I was. I felt sore no matter what I did. I drove Jionni crazy tossing and turning. On top of that, I had to pee every hour on the hour. It felt like a leprechaun was dancing on my bladder.

Leaks. Break out the Depends! If I laughed, I leaked. If I sneezed, I wet myself. Coughed? Like I sat in a puddle. For three months, I was changing my granny panties every few hours. A girlfriend of mine with two kids told me she peed herself constantly. Even now, three years after giving birth, every time she jumps, she dribbles a bit. Another friend told me to do Kegels to help with pushing during labor. Good idea. I had to get toned. Whenever I peed, I squeezed to stop the flow. I really bulked up my vag muscles. I have no idea if it helped during labor, but now I can run, jump, laugh, sneeze, and cough without self-wetting. Before bed, I still do twenty minutes of squeezing, and now I'm practically a juicehead down there.

Weird discharge. At around week 35, I woke up one morning with a big stain on my shirt at boob level. Milk?! It was too early for that. Later in the day, I decided to play around and squeezed my boob. A thick, yellowish drop oozed out of my nipple. I'd read about this gunk. It was called colostrum, aka starter milk. It was happening! My mammary glands were kicking into production for Lorenzo, and now I had my own milk service, my personal dairy farm. I hoped the early sign of colostrum meant I'd go into labor earlier than my due date.

Shortness of breath. My uterus pressed on all my other organs, including my stomach. Throwing up in my mouth was a daily occurrence. My lungs were reduced to the size of a bunch of grapes. I'd lose my breath just watching TV. Walking up the stairs was like running a 5K. Thank God I had Jionni's muscular arms pushing my pregnant ass up the stairs or I would have been stuck in the basement for weeks.

Grouchies. Besides the bloat, zits, tonnage, exhaustion, and soreness, I felt FREAKIN' AWESOME! Until I didn't. One gas pain, and I'd hate everything. I felt helpless and depressed at the end. I couldn't move, relax, or sit still. Heartburn ruined eating, and the pain made me unpleasant company. I just didn't want to be near people, but I was surrounded all the time. I had a camera following me—except to the bathroom, where I went every ten minutes. I just wanted to be alone to cry by myself. I couldn't wait for this to be over. If I really wanted to freak myself out, I'd imagine going past my due date by weeks. The thought made me burst into tears. Jionni cheered me up, though. He just kept assuring me we'd get through it and that we'd be great parents.

Baby movements. If I had to come up with one positive physical experience during my last trimester, it would be how Lorenzo treated my uterus like a punching bag. I know, that doesn't sound good. It could hurt, but I loved it. It meant Enzo was alive and kicking. When he squirmed into a head-down position, his skull right against my pelvic bones, I could actually see his other body parts. A foot. A hand. His cute butt. Even though his movements made me nauseated, I loved watching my alien squirm around in my belly. Every punch was like a private conversation, just the two of us.

I told myself, "Embrace this now. You'll definitely miss this feeling until the next pregnancy."

Chapter 15

Labor Day

In August, people started saying, "You're going to go any minute." I wish! I'd been ready for months to meet Lorenzo and end the hell that was pregnancy. But I was still two weeks away from my due date. The one time it wasn't rude to arrive early was childbirth. As soon as I crossed the 36-week hurdle—when the baby was considered full term—I begged Lorenzo to make his move. I'd yell at my belly, "Get out of there already!"

Two weeks and a day before my due date, I was sick as a dog. Jionni's family came over to have a barbecue. Everyone was hanging out, having a ball in the kitchen (where else?). I could barely talk to anyone. I left the room and sat by myself on the deck. It was a perfect summer day, but a black cloud hung over my head. People left me alone. They knew to let me sit by myself and wallow in my misery. Yet being apart from the group but still in sight wasn't enough. I had to get away. Hearing their happy voices made me feel worse. Nothing feels lonelier than listening to other people laugh when you feel like crying.

I went to the basement to be by myself. Jionni came down and gave me the encouragement I needed. I know he wished he could take my pain and sadness on himself to give me a break. But as much as he wanted to, he couldn't be pregnant for me. Technology hasn't come that far. Maybe by the time we're planning our fourth.

The bad day turned into a horrendous night. I couldn't sleep at all. I got out of bed around 4:00 AM, beyond uncomfortable. It felt like I had peed myself, or like I got my period, which wasn't possible. I Kegeled like a champ, but the trickle didn't let up. It occurred to me that my water might have broken, but it was just a trickle. I hauled my whale body to the bathroom (where else?). When I wiped, this gross thing was on the toilet paper. It looked like a condom had fallen out of my vagina.

Of course, I freaked and made Jionni get up and look at the booger creature.

"Is it the mucus plug?" I asked, holding it up for him to see.

"Mucus, yes," he shouted. "Now get that out of my face."

We shouted "mucus" a few more times, just because. How many opportunities in life do you get to scream "mucus"?

The cervical cork had definitely unplugged. There it was in a wad of toilet paper. But I still wasn't sure my water had broken. For months, I'd pictured a huge waterfall gushing out. Remember the scene in *Titanic* when the ship hit the iceberg and water exploded into the hull? Like that, but from the vagina. Welp, that didn't happen to me. It just dribbled down my leg.

We called the doctor and described what was going on. He said, "Sounds like your water broke. It's not always a gush. Just sit tight until your contractions are five minutes apart."

First lesson: You don't always get the labor you dreamed about or pictured in your head. We had to deal with what was actually happening. And it was really happening. The time had finally come. The agonizing and uncomfortable nine months were all going to be worth it when I pushed out my little bundle, and it was going to happen very, very soon.

HELLO, NERVES!

Here's Jionni

The mucus plug was nasty. She didn't have to show it to me. That was unnecessary.

Baby Bumps

My advice to ladies is not to make your man look at it. But that was the proof Nicole was going into labor. I felt excited and nervous. We'd been waiting nine months for this. The last month or two had taken a toll on everyone. Now that it was finally happening, I did run through some worst- and best-case scenarios. A lot went through my mind. But when I found myself imagining things, I would stop and make myself focus on what was actually happening. There was no point in worrying about what could happen. It calmed me down to stay in the moment and ask myself and Nicole, "What can I do now to help?"

In another hour, I started to get serious pain. It felt like period cramps, but much worse. That was when I thought, *That has got to be a real contraction.* They were ten minutes apart. It went on like that for hours. I couldn't wait anymore, so in the morning we went to the doctor to confirm that I was leaking amniotic fluid. My cervix, though, was being a lazy bitch and not doing anything. It hadn't opened at all. The doc sent us back home to rest until a room at the hospital was available. For some reason, everyone in Jersey was popping out guidos that day.

Talk about torture. The worst thing about the whole labor process wasn't the pain. It was the waiting to meet my baby. That whole morning, I kept trickling fluid like I was peeing myself. I killed time doing my makeup and hair. I got myself dolled up, like I was going out to dinner. I made sure to use extra glue on my lashes. It wouldn't look good if they fell off and poked me in the eye while I was pushing out Lorenzo. My hospital outfit—a leopard print nightie—was clean and ready to go. You never get a second chance to make a first impression. I wanted to look good for Lorenzo. If I could have someone in the delivery room doing makeup touchups, I would! Just a little powder on my nose between pushes, thanks!

We'd done a dry run to the hospital the week before. It was hectic and messy. Jionni got lost on the way there. We'd been there like 500 times before, but it took us an hour to go four miles. If our dry run was anything like the real deal, I might've given birth in the car and had a backseat baby.

Actually, that dry run wasn't so dry. I peed myself on the way there.

When it was the real deal, Jionni and I headed over in the late afternoon, a full thirteen hours after my water broke. He was a rock. He didn't run around like a chicken with his head cut off, throw the suitcase into the car, and then speed off, forgetting his panting wife in the driveway. He was relaxed. The ride was quiet and calm. If you were watching from the outside, you might think it was *too* calm. Inside my head, I was quaking with fear. My teeth were chattering. I'd read about labor and delivery. I'd heard the stories. But I hadn't experienced it. It was a huge unknown. I'm very sensitive to physical pain. If I get a shot or a bruise, it really kills. Contractions and pushing were supposed to be like no other pain in the world. The contractions so far had felt like my lower half was a rope, twisting hard. And it was just the beginning! It would only get worse as my cervix dilated.

Yeah, I was scared! Terrified.

Once we were admitted and in the room, a nurse asked if we wanted to do our Lamaze breathing. No, thanks! Jionni and I did go to a Lamaze class to see what it was about. We learned how to do a "cleansing breath," and other, dirtier breaths. Whatevs. It was confusing and seemed pointless. Lamaze is for people who wanted to do natural childbirth without pain medication. Well, I planned on loading up on whatever they could give me. Pain relief was totally safe for the baby and me. Why be in agony by choice? I didn't get that. After five minutes of Lamaze, we knew it wasn't for us. The other couple took it so seriously. We kept cracking up, and they just stared at us. Cricket city. I tried to hold in the giggles, but that made it even funnier. We didn't want to disrespect the teacher, but the pictures of the women giving birth in different positions looked like a fetish Kama Sutra. When she pointed out the woman giving birth on all fours like a cow on the farm, we just couldn't stop laughing. I nearly peed myself. FYI: I wound up holding my breath during my delivery. No cleansing breath or he-he-heing. I was fine. When you're in the moment, I doubt breathing a certain way would lessen the pain at all.

I liked my hospital bed. I was as comfy as possible. My parents arrived. Jenni and Roger drove up. They'd all come for the birth. The reality of the situation hit me. I started freaking out. Would I have pain? What was going to happen next? Some people had a nightmare experience. For others, it was a piece of cake. How would it go for me? Would my vagina stretch out permanently? Sex with me afterward might be like throwing a stick in the ocean. Would I have postpartum depression? Would Lorenzo be okay? What if I were a horrible mother? Now, I get it that worry was part of the motherhood package. I would worry about Lorenzo every day for the rest of my life. But right then, I was pretty much terrified of the pain.

Jionni managed to break through the fear, making me laugh. He knew he had to hold it together, that if he freaked out, I would, too. Neither of us wanted that to happen. He was probably just as nervous and scared as I was. One thing I never worried about during the entire nine months was whether Jionni would be a great dad. I tried to calm my nerves by playing Christmas music.

Another two hours went by. My mucus plug came out fifteen hours before, but my cervix had dilated only one centimeter. It would have to yawn another nine centimeters before I could push. To make me open faster, the doctor wanted to insert a balloon and force my cervix to dilate and to give me Pitocin, a drug that would increase contractions—and pain. At this point, they felt like period cramps times one thousand. They'd get worse? He asked, "Do you want the balloon or the epidural first?"

Let's see . . . agonizing pain or sweet relief? How would I choose?

"This isn't rocket science, doc!" I said. "Give me the epidural!"

Have I mentioned that I'm terrified of needles? This was the one time I was glad to see it coming. The epidural didn't really hurt. It was a weird feeling to know a huge needle was in my spine. Once the drugs kicked in, I was numb from the waist down. If the epidural were a person, I would seriously hug the shit out of her for helping me through the some of the scariest moments of my life. The pain just stopped. Bzzip. My vagina was cold as an iceberg. It felt awesome. I pushed down on my belly and I couldn't feel a thing. But would that work? Could I push with an iceberg vagina? I might not have pain now, but what about during? Or after? The pain was gone, but the nerves were still there.

The doctor did the balloon and gave me the Pitocin to make the contractions harder. It still took forever to dilate. My body and mind weren't ready to open up. Another five, six, ten hours went by. We chilled on the bed, watching cartoons. I took a nap, and woke up. The nurse checked my progress. "I'll just take a looksee in your vag for a second . . ." My cervix was still taking its motherfucking time. I thought about Lorenzo, warm and cozy, and hoped he was enjoying his last couple hours in there.

It was now 26 hours since my water broke. I really had to take a shit.

"I have to go to the bathroom," I told the doctor. *"Right now."* I asked to be carried to the bathroom because I was going to poop all over the hospital bed.

"That means you're ready to push," said the doctor.

"No," I said. It really felt like I had to take a serious shit.

He took a look. "It's time," he said. "Start pushing!"

A day of waiting, and now I wished I had another minute to get ready. "I can't do it!" I screamed. "What the fuck! I'm never doing this again!"

I had *never* been so nervous in my life. I shivered like I was in Antarctica in a bikini. But I knew there was only one way this was going to end. I found my last ounce of strength.

"Let's do this!" I said. Lorenzo was ready to enter the world. I would be, too.

Jionni was up at my head, and my mom held my legs. I cried even though I wasn't in pain. I just held my breath and bore down. If you love pooping like me, and consider yourself an expert in that area, pushing will be a piece of cake for you. I pushed only about eight times and my baby came out!

Lorenzo Dominic LaValle was born on August 26, 2012, at 3:10 in the morning. Six pounds and five ounces. The national holiday was a week later, but that date will always be Labor Day for me.

What a huge relief it was to push him out! I just felt pressure, like shitting out a dinoturd. Speaking of . . . I felt sure I was going to crap while pushing. But I didn't. Thank Gawd! It's no big deal, but I didn't want to have my birth experience marred by smelling my own shit. I did fart in the doctor's face, but I didn't even know I was doing it because of the numbness. It either happens or not, but you can't control it. He basically ate my fart. "I don't mind. It happens all the time," he said. Just the same, sorry about that, Doc!

Here's Jionni

Being there for the birth of my son was an amazing experience. I have no words for it. I was up by Nicole's head. I didn't watch Lorenzo come out of her body. I got advice not to watch, that it'd scar me for life. I thought I could handle it, but I didn't want to risk it. Maybe next time.

I was worried about Lorenzo, but the doctor was right there for him. I was also concerned for Nicole. Throughout the pregnancy, at each check up, she screamed and cried when she was just touched a little. So I had some doubts about how she'd be during labor. But she was aweseome. She just pushed our boy out, one, two, three. It was incredible. I couldn't have done it. I was so proud of her. It definitely made me fall even more in love.

They put Lorenzo on my chest. I cried, laughed, and yelled, "I love you!" He was finally here in my arms, all slimy and covered in blood. I've done a lot of crazy things in my life, but *nothing* will ever compare to the moment of giving birth to my child and meeting him for the first time. This little baby was a part of me and he will forever bring love and happiness into our lives. So trust me, ladies, all the anxiety, nerves, pain, and torture you endure throughout your pregnancy and labor is all worth it to finally hold your baby. I can honestly say I cannot wait to have more babies! Lorenzo stared at me, and I cried about how perfect he was. A lot of new moms don't bond immediately with their baby. I was relieved to feel the burst of love at first sight with Lorenzo. Just instantaneous, mad, crazy, fierce, incredible love.

"That was it?" I asked. "I can do that again."

The nurses cracked up. Ten minutes ago, I was screaming, "I can't!! Never again!"

I'd waited so long, and had been through so much for this moment. Lorenzo and I had been together the whole time, but now separated, we were truly united. Jionni cut the umbilical cord. One more push for the placenta, which slithered out. Jionni described it later, saying, "Galloons of blood gushed into the pan. It was sloppy and wet and looked like a big bloody stingray with a tail." He was probably traumatized for life.

The doctor asked if I wanted to see the placenta. He cut it in half and showed me how it worked. I grew an extra organ to make Lorenzo. When I didn't need it anymore, it came sliding out. Amazing. As incredible as it was, I had no intention of eating it like a ham steak, or putting it in a blender and drinking it. People do that! Or they use it for shampoo. Seriously, it's an alien. It's out of this world. Eating it? No freakin' way! Yuck.

Since I gave birth, a lot of people have asked me questions about pregnancy and labor. I can tell that they are scared shitless about what's going to happen to them. Let me tell you, I am the biggest baby you will ever meet when it comes to pain, and I was a fucking champ during labor. You have no idea how nervous I was. If you saw *Snooki & JWOWW* Season Two, they showed part of my labor. I was crying with my lip quivering. That's not even half of it, ladies. It's terrifying to think that a 6-to-9-pound baby is going to squeeze out of your vagina. It's seriously a miracle that we can do it, but we do.

When the time comes to step up to the plate and push that baby out, you are going to be ready and do a fantastic job. I just want to get across that it's normal and *okay* to be scared. You have no idea what to expect. Trust me, you are stronger than you think. When the moment comes to be brave, you will be. You will tolerate the pain. You'll still be nervous. But bravery will overcome that. Once it's all over, you'll say, "Piece of cake!" You'll feel like Super Woman. Let's be honest, all of us who give birth are Super Women. We are straight-up strong ass bosses. No one is going to fuck with us.

Chapter 16

Firsts

———∞———

During the first month, every day was full of "firsts." Every hour! It was all brand-spanking new. (Wonder where that phrase came from? In the old days, the doctor held the newborn upside down by the ankles and spanked his ass to get him crying/breathing. Now the doc suctions the mucus out of the baby's mouth and he starts breathing on his own. With Lorenzo, it happened so fast, I didn't even see it.) Some of motherhood came naturally, right away. Right from the start, I instinctually knew how to hold him and talk to him. But I had a lot to learn.

Along with the firsts, I had a lot of second guessing. Lorenzo's first month, for Jionni and me, was a trial by shit storm. We had to figure it all out ASAP, or fail our baby—not an option.

Some of our firsts were predictable. Some we didn't see coming. It didn't matter. A first is a first, and once it was over, we considered our cherries popped. I can't remember it chronologically. It went by in a flash. I barely changed out of my pajamas for weeks. Motherhood scrambled my sense of time. We were up all night, and slept—when we could—during the day. The baby wasn't on a schedule, and neither were we. Highlights from our month of firsts:

First look. I'd seen glimpses of Lorenzo in the sonograms. But it wasn't like laying eyes on him in the flesh. I'd been waiting so long. What would he look like? Waiting to see him made me nuts with anticipation. Why did pregnancy take so friggin' *long*? I admit, I was scared he'd be an ugly newborn, like those shriveled old man babies. But he wasn't. That first second I saw him, he was covered in blood and mucus. He also looked a bit blue. After a minute, he got red (only to turn yellow the next day from jaundice). They wiped him off, and I held him. I stared at my boy, and thought, *You're mine! I love you!* He looked a lot like Jionni, same nose. But now I see the combination of the two of us in Lorenzo's face. It was instant love, instant protectiveness. Then the nurses tried to take him away. I was like, "Where the fuck are you going? You're not taking my baby anywhere!" Mama Bear mode kicked in right away. The claws came out.

First molestation. And the second, and the third, and the hundredth. Get ready to be molested by everyone in the hospital. Post-birth was the worst part for me. That's when the drugs wore off and my body had to deal with the pain and recovery of pushing a baby out of my vag. At first, I felt a little weird having everyone check my vagina and asshole to see if it was bleeding, but by the third nurse dabbing my vagina, I was over it. You also have multiple nurses squeezing your tits to help with the milk and breast-feeding process. Jionni freaked out at first because everyone in the hospital came in to feel my jugs. I had to reassure him that they do that to EVERYONE, not just because the whole staff wanted to see "Snooki's tits." You will have to share your goods with the hospital. Eventually, you'll get used to it and say, "Fuck it. Just do what you gotta do."

First panic. Lorenzo was born with jaundice, which happens to a lot of newborns. Basically, his liver wasn't working up to speed after relying on the placenta to do its job for so long. It can take a baby a few days to get it right. In the meantime, his eyes and skin can look a little yellow. Jionni and I were assured this is normal, and not a cause for concern. We freaked out anyway. Even when the nurses said it was no big deal, any mention that the baby wasn't one thousand percent healthy was like an ice pick to the chest. I asked them over and over, "He's okay, right?" He was fine. The treatment was exposure to sunlight. Lorenzo was put under lights that looked like food warmers. Baby's first tanning session! When we left the hospital after a few days, we made sure to get him into the sun. When the jaundice went away, we could see his natural skin tone shining through. He was a guido all the way.

Our *second* major panic came months later, when Lorenzo got an ear infection and a fever. Again, totally normal and easily treated. But I couldn't stand to see my boy in pain! We didn't want him to suffer, but throwing antibiotics at him wasn't the way to build up his immune system. So we comforted him as best we could while he fought it off himself. That was a rough few days. Definitely more painful for us than for him.

First cut. We decided to do the circumcision. A boy should look like his daddy. Also, why saddle him with the risk of smegma? Totally vile! Who would want to be his girlfriend if his penis smelled like cheese or looked weird? The doctor wouldn't let us watch, which was fine with me. I didn't want to see Lorenzo cry. "Just the foreskin, not the whole tip," we said to the doctor. To Lorenzo, we said, "Bye bye, weiner!" and he was taken away. Jionni had sympathetic pain. I noticed him holding himself.

They came back five minutes later.

"That was so short!" I said.

"Hey, that's my boy you're talking about," said Jionni.

The doctor showed us the foreskin in a jar. It was just a tiny scrap of skin, already shrinking. I thought, *That'd be a cool keepsake!* I wanted to save it all. A lock of newborn hair, all his teeth. I would have had his first poop bronzed, with actual bronze. (Jionni said no.)

I asked, "Can we keep the foreskin? I really like scrapbooking."

"Uh, no," the doctor said.

He didn't let us have it. I can't fault the guy; he did such a great job. Lorenzo's penis looked awesome. He's going to have a great life with that thing.

We did keep the umbilical cord stump. It fell off after a week. We put it in a jar. It looked like a bacon strip. I'll break that out when Lorenzo is sixteen. "Here's where we were attached," I'll say. He'll groan or say, "That's disgusting, Mom."

First PITA (Pain in the Ass) moment. I was probably the most annoying new mom they ever had in that hospital. I rang the nurses every five minutes to come to our room and answer questions.

"Is it okay if he hiccups?"

"Can he sleep on his back?"

"Can we use hair gel on him?"

Seriously, we knew NOTHING. It's one thing to read about this stuff, and another thing to do it all. We were so ridiculously clueless.

The nurse would come in again, and I'd just crack up thinking how big a pain in the ass I was. But whenever I laughed, my vagina hurt.

Jionni asked the lactation consultant, "If Nicole eats chocolate, will she give chocolate milk?" He was busting her ass, but she didn't realize. I guess, in a way, it could be a legit question. Like, would the milk have a lot of sugar in it? Every time we rang the buzzer, we apologized for being annoying. They told us, "All new parents have a million questions. Keep asking. There's no such thing as a stupid question." We kept the stupid coming every few minutes for three days.

First outing. We left the protective bubble of the hospital, and it was terrifying! I was afraid to take Lorenzo into the big, bad world. I held him tight, all bundled up. I wasn't going to let anyone hurt him. I sat in the back of the car with Lorenzo in his new infant car seat while Jionni drove us home. When the sun came in through the window, I put my shades on his face. He looked adorable! I loved my little man so much already, it hurt.

First awww. We arrived back at the house, and carried our boy down the steps. Remember, I was two weeks early. We'd planned on using that time to set up his crib and stuff. As we walked down the steps to the basement, we expected to find the place a mess. But it was beautiful! While we were at the hospital, Jionni's mom spent days getting our apartment in shape. She unpacked all the baby stuff and assembled the crib and changing table. She even hung up the letters of Lorenzo's name over the crib. It was so sweet! I am so grateful to her, and all of our parents, for being the best grandparents ever. Lorenzo is blessed!

First waaa. Forget it! I cried constantly. I never cried before (well, hardly ever). But I sobbed when Lorenzo was born. I got misty whenever I held him or looked at him. My boy was my first blood, and I couldn't help crying at how beautiful and perfect he was. I cried when Jionni and I fought, when my breasts hurt, when I felt frustrated or tired. If Lorenzo cried—which wasn't that often, my good baby—I did, too. When he got baptized, I was a mess. I could have filled the holy water basin with my own tears. Being a mom has turned me into a wet tissue. I cry when I see other women with their babies now. It's insane. I was making up for years of being buttoned up and not letting it flow. You give birth, and every blocked emotion comes streaming out along with the baby.

First day home. It was so exciting. When Lorenzo peeped, Jionni and I jumped up, giggling, and rushed to the crib. We ran through the checklist. Is he hungry? Wet? Bored? Gassy? We didn't want to miss a minute of it. Since Lorenzo raged all night like his parents used to, there were a lot of minutes. If I thought I was tired during the first trimester, it was nothing compared to this. Even though I loved it, surviving on no sleep made it hard to function. Down was up, up was down, day was night. I had no idea what was going on. After a day or two, we thought it'd be smarter to take shifts. I was a night owl, so I'd take the nights. Jionni was an early riser, so he would do days. But that didn't work either. We both wanted to do it all, and got up together anyway. That lasted about a month. Then we hit a wall of exhaustion. Now, we beg each other to get up.

First temper tantrum. Mine. On no sleep, a person can get cranky. I eventually got used to it. But the first few weeks of sleep deprivation were *torture*. My baby was an enhanced interrogation technique. A few times, I caught myself yelling at him, "Go the fuck to sleep!" Then I'd be horrified by my outburst and apologize. "I'm sorry," I said. "Mommy's just bone freakin' tired." I felt really bad afterward. If I let the baby cry, I felt like a terrible parent. One time, I yelled, "I don't know why the fuck you're crying!" He got louder. Lorenzo was trying to say, "You're being an asshole, Mommy." That was the last time I yelled. It does get aggravating. But raising your voice doesn't help. A baby can't understand your frustration. If I'd been trying to calm him for an hour, and I needed a break before I punched myself in the face,

I put him down, walked away, and caught my breath. Then I could go back and feel ready for it.

First poop. I mean mine. Friends warned me that the first poop after giving birth was like shitting a ball of barbed wire. Kewl. It would definitely hurt my tender parts. It was a massacre down there. I bent over with a mirror to see. I had three stitches. (Unless you're a raging whore with a Grand Canyon kookah, you will rip or get cut.) It looked like I'd torn a second vagina. Taking a dump would be like tearing a second anus. It was still really sore, too. I didn't eat the day I gave birth and not much of anything the day after. So I didn't have to face this battle until the fourth day. I had to psyche myself up like a soldier going into battle. I entered the bathroom, aka my torture chamber. I sat down, gripped the rim with both hands, and struggled with it. I wasn't afraid of popping a hemorrhoid anymore. But I was afraid to tear my stitches. I'd had a baby. I'd been to the bloody wars. In the end, I got it out. It might sound crazy, but this was a *huge* accomplishment. I felt like a weight was taken off my . . . butthole? I might've cried with relief. My ass hurt for hours after, though.

First diaper change. Again, I mean me! After giving birth, you aren't allowed to just wipe with normal toilet paper. You have to spray yourself down with an iodine wash to clean the stitches, then pat dry

Lorenzo's First Year

Lorenzo's first minutes in a comfortable cocoon.

I could stare at him forever while he sleeps. He's beautiful.

We're basically twins!

With my twin in the morning.

Mommy loves you
forever and ever.
You'll always be my baby.

Bathing in the
sink!

My Christmas present!

He didn't cry with Santa Claus. That's my boy!

Our first Christmas picture. Many more to come through the years, and I can't wait.

Ringing in 2013 with my family! So much better than being drunk at a club. Oh, how times change!

When Lorenzo started smiling,
it was amazing.
Now he doesn't stop smiling!
He's such a happy baby.

Sleeping Beauty

My baby was so tiny! Time flies!

Family vacation in Florida—Lorenzo is 4 months old.

I'm not just saying this 'cause he's my baby, but I have the **CUTEST** baby ever!

My little business man!

with special cold wipes. It was a ten-minute routine every time I peed. I wore brick-sized pads that had to be changed every hour. My lady parts ached for days, so I put ice cubes on the pad to numb them.

Lorenzo's first diaper change. We put it on backwards. Not that it mattered. He splattered it with his yellow curds five seconds later, and we had to do it all over again. I worried I'd be grossed out (I didn't have a good track record when it came to changing diapers), but I loved Lorenzo's poop. So did Jionni. We fought over who got to change him.

First look at myself naked. Scary! I got fat while pregnant, yeah. My attitude was, *So what?* I knew I'd take it off later, after the baby was born. Well, later had arrived. I'd given birth, but my belly was still round. I still had hot flashes, felt sore, and was leaking crazy fluids. Pregnancy hormones had made my hair thick during the pregnancy. Now they were diminishing and my hair was falling out! The shower drain looked like it was clogged with a guinea pig. The bloat from water retention was going down. I had the soaking wet sheets from night sweats to prove it. But I still felt huge. My engorged boobs were absurd. If I auditioned for a porn movie, the director would say, "Sorry, hon, but your tits are too big." That big. My belly sagged like a punctured soccer ball. I could store a week's groceries in my mommy pouch. The stretch marks on my boobs and belly were red and angry.

They weren't going away anytime soon. I was only 25. I thought my body would bounce right back. Wrong. I don't care how young you are. You need to have realistic expectations. I did manage to get myself back into shape—the best shape of my life, in fact—but I had to bust my ass to do it over a period of many months. (More on that later.)

First escape. My first hour of Me Time? I got my nails done. Jionni stayed home to feed and burp the baby. I felt guilty being away from Lorenzo, and called home to check in. As it turned out, Jionni took some Me Time, too, playing football in the yard and letting his mom do all the work. I didn't care about that. But Jionni lied. He said he was feeding Lorenzo when he wasn't. Sneaky hubbie. I forgave him.

First flirt. A week or so postpartum, the sexy feeling was slowly creeping back. We couldn't have sex for six weeks, but I still wanted to cuddle! I was counting down the days until we could get it on. I tried flirting with Jionni. Making eyes and leaning on him. He was totally into Lorenzo and barely looked at me! I whined about not getting enough cuddling time. Looking back, it was odd how much I wanted him when I couldn't do it. But when we finally could have sex, I wasn't remotely in the mood. We didn't get around to that for a few months.

First smoke. I blame Jionni's mom's sangria, which she keeps in an enormous cooler on the kitchen counter. The sangria taunted me for nine months of pregnancy. One day when my friend Stephanie was visiting, I had my first cup of it. I got a tiny buzz, and that made me want to have a cigarette.

I bought a pack. It was an impulse purchase. I stopped smoking with the snap of my fingers when I realized I was pregnant. I wasn't really a diehard smoker anyway, it was just something I did when drinking. Welp, the pregnancy was over. I'd been so good for so long! I had no intention of smoking regularly, but I wanted to do something a little bit bad.

I knew Jionni wouldn't approve. I'd never smoke anywhere near my baby, but I didn't want to get in trouble with my fiancé for smoking at all. So I waited until he went out. My mom watched Lorenzo while Stephanie and I went outside for a cigarette. The first inhale was kind of disgusting. It stank! Did cigarettes always smell so foul? I was paranoid the smoke would get in my hair and clothes. I had like two drags before I put it out and went inside to take a shower.

The guilt! It felt like I had killed someone. I ended up confessing to Jionni.

His turn to get pissed off. He felt lied to. "What kind of fiancée are you? I don't care if you have one cigarette, but don't go behind my back," he said. I learned my lesson. I promised him, from that point on, I would tell him whenever I did something wrong. That promise would bite me hard in the ass soon enough.

First spray. I tanned after a few weeks. It was like spraying on the pretty and brought me back to life. Mommies have to make time for themselves. Once a month, I take a day to get a tan, get my nails done, and have my hair done. I go to lunch or shop with friends. One day a month isn't too much to ask for a happy state of mind. I want to be with Lorenzo and do everything for him. In order to be present and in the moment with him 97 percent of the time, I need my 3 percent of Me Time. You care for your baby by caring for yourself.

First night out with Jionni. You had to care for the relationship, too. Jenni and Roger babysat so Jionni and I could go out to dinner, have a couple's night, and get some romance back. We brought a bottle of white wine along. My first sip? Blecch. It tasted funny. My tongue wasn't used to the flavor. Just to confirm, I had another sip, and another. Two glasses later, I started giggling, then snorting, then crying about how much I loved my baby. I was right back on that hormonal, emotional roller coaster. Maybe I was a little drunkie, too. Jionni said, "She's back."

Meh. It didn't feel like a return to my old self, though. That girl was gone (and by "gone," I don't mean wasted). When I watched the scene on *Snooki & JWOWW* Season Two, I noticed something I didn't realize at the time. During the entire meal, Jionni and I talked about Lorenzo. We were out, alone together for the first time in a month, and we couldn't stop obsessing about what was happening at home. When we got back to the house, we both ran down the stairs, and said, "Where's my boy?" We chased Jenni and Roger away so we could fuss over the baby. Jionni looked at me and said, "I can't believe we have a kid."

More giggling and crying.

It's been months since that night. We talk about other things now. The laser focus on Lorenzo has softened. But whenever we go out, we're counting the minutes until we get back home. We were two. Now, we're three. It's not that Jionni and I are bored with each other. But we're both *really* into Lorenzo. Like, really into him. I'd missed people before. When I had boyfriend, for example, I felt depressed to be apart, even for a little while. None of that compared to the . . .

First night apart. I waited until Lorenzo was four months old and went to Los Angeles to do press for *Snooki & JWOWW*. But I couldn't sleep. I was worried sick and wondering how he was doing. In the hotel, I slept like a baby all right—up ever few hours, crying. It physically hurt to be separated from him, like a body part had been detached. Every chance I got, I would FaceTime with Jionni and have him hold up the phone to Lorenzo just so I could see him and he could hear my voice. As soon as we hung up, though, the waterworks started all over again. Anything would set me off. A TV commercial about dogs. A Taylor Swift song. Other mothers with their kids. I'm not doing long trips anymore, not if I can help it. I just can't do it. Longing for Lorenzo takes too much out of me.

Chapter 17

'd heard and read that breast milk had the most nutrients and was best for the baby. So that's what I wanted to give Lorenzo. Nothing but the best. But I'd also heard from a friend that breastfeeding hurt like a *mother*, which I guess was appropriate.

I have the pain tolerance of a mosquito, and I was hesitant to have my nipple sucked off. But I tried it anyway. Things didn't go so smoothly. I grabbed Lorenzo by the back of the head like they taught me at the hospital, and shoved his tiny face into my ginormous boob. The poor kid didn't stand a chance. His lips were searching and pursing, but it took forever for him to latch on the right way. But then he'd get detached and we had to start the nipple hunt all over again. Meanwhile, I was rearranging him, cursing and sweating. Jionni encouraged me. His saying, "Come on, you can do it," didn't really help. I felt like a complete failure for not getting the hang of it. I was determined to keep trying. "Breast is best! Breast is best!" I kept muttering. They might as well have piped that into the PA system at the hospital.

After we brought Lorenzo home, the latching on problems continued. No matter how I held his head, my boobs smothered him. His lips were too small to hang onto my nipples. We had a baby scale to check Lorenzo's growth. Every day, he lost a little weight. I doubled down trying to get him to latch onto my twin planetoids. They got bigger and bigger, but the baby was shrinking. My frustration? Through the roof.

"This isn't working," I said, freaking out. "Lorenzo isn't eating."

"He's fine," said Jionni, annoyingly calm. "Try it again."

I sat down on the couch, and repeated the routine I was taught—position boob, position baby head, contact, adjust—for *an hour*. My breasts were engorged to skin-splitting fullness. Some milk dribbled out. But Lorenzo. Would. Not. Latch. I weighed him obsessively, like every hour. When his weight dropped another half an ounce, I started crying. "We have to give him a bottle," I said. He wasn't eating enough, and the more I panicked, the worse it got.

Breast is best, breast is best . . .

For me, breastfeeding was the worst. Jionni wanted me to keep going. If you give a baby a bottle too soon, he'll get the dreaded "nipple confusion" and never learn to latch on the right way. But I'd had enough. "Fuck it," I said, and just gave him baby formula. He slurped it down. He was obviously starving. Never again would I let my baby go hungry.

I stopped shoving his face against my chest, and broke out the Medela breast pump I got from my baby shower. From that moment, I sucked the milk out of my udders with a machine—both at once—for 15 minutes every three hours for the next three months. I took my pump everywhere. Women had told me that, when they looked at their baby or even at a photo of their baby, their boobs leaked milk. When I looked at my pump or even a photo of it (I kept one in my wallet next to Lorenzo's—kidding!), the milk faucets opened. Breastfeeding was, truly, a beautiful bonding experience. I grew to love my pump on a deep level.

It hurt at first. But after the first couple hard tugs of suction, it actually felt good to pump. It was a huge relief to get the milk out of my engorged ducts. The sucking action wasn't continuous like a vacuum cleaner. It was rhythmic, just like taking alternate tugs on a cow's nipples, one then the other, spraying into the bucket, or the bottle attachment. The intensity of the suction was adjustable. I kept it low for the first few minutes, and then slowly increased it to get the milk out faster. When it was on High Suck, my nipple would get as long and red as a grape. Not appetizing. They had three hours to calm down, and then the Girls and I would go at it all over again.

At full engorgement, my breasts were rock hard with milk. It felt like I was hauling a pair of bowling balls in my bra. If anything set them off, it was Niagara Falls on my shirt. Wet circles would seep through my clothes. I was shopping with Jenni at Mandee once during filming, and I had to ask the salesgirl for a paper towel to put in my bra before I tried on any clothes. It was the right thing to do and probably saved me some money. They have a store policy: If you milk on it, you buy it.

I figured it didn't matter how Lorenzo was getting my milk, as long as he was getting it. In an ideal world, he would have latched on perfectly. It wouldn't have hurt. We would have bonded magically. He would have sucked like a boss and we would have kept it up for a year. But that wasn't how things played out. I milked myself for my baby. I made sure he got what he needed in a way that made sense for us. I definitely enjoyed burning a zillion calories a day (okay, more like 500) by manufacturing all that milk. So I didn't do it the traditional way. So what? If people had any objections to that, they could SUCK IT!

Meanwhile, the greatest invention ever is the hands-free breast pump bra. I loved this. I'd slip the funnels into the bra and turn on the pump. I'd hang out on the couch, watching TV with a cold drink, flipping through magazines, and meanwhile, the pump just kept siphoning away. If a Martian flew down from outer space, landed in our basement and got a load of me filing my nails while a machine sucked white fluid out of my chest, he'd think, *Earth people are friggin' cray-cray. I'm outta here.* I said to Jionni, "I could throw on the backpack and my new bra, and walk around the malls, shopping and milking myself at the same time." He did NOT love that idea.

A major complicating factor of pumping: We were filming Season Two of *Snooki & JWOWW*. I had to cover my boobs when I was hooked up to the machine or lock myself in the bathroom where cameras weren't allowed to go. I was thrilled when the season wrapped so I could air out my boobs whenever and wherever I wanted.

By the time Lorenzo was a few weeks old, I was pumping like a badass cow, producing all the milk he needed, and then some. We had extra to freeze for future use. Jionni said, "Why don't you try breastfeeding again?" Pumping and then feeding did double the workload. Feeding him straight from the boob would remove a time-consuming step. By then, I was a lot more relaxed about the whole thing. The baby was a lot stronger and heavier after a month, and my boobs weren't quite as gargantuan as when my milk first came in.

"Okay," I said.

I put Lorenzo's lips up to my nipple, and he latched on! I looked up at Jionni, tears in my eyes. We finally did it! No nipple confusion for my boy.

Lorenzo started sucking—*hard*. And my tears started flowing. My friend hadn't been kidding. It killed! I doubled over in pain. "He's ripping my nipple off!"

Jionni said, "That's my boy!"

Huh? A father proud of his son for attacking his mother's nipples? Not cool. I de-latched, and gave Lorenzo a bottle.

After months of watching Lorenzo guzzle my breast milk like it was divine fluid of the gods, I started getting curious about the taste. I heard about a restaurant in Manhattan that actually serves human milk to put in your coffee. My first reaction was that they'd have to pay me to drink that! Then again, maybe human milk tasted just like cow's milk. Only one way to find out.

I didn't actually sample my goods, though, until one night when Roger, Jenni's fiancé, dared us each to do a shot of my milk. I figured, how gross could it be? It came out of my body. Then again, shit came out of my body, too, and I wasn't going to chow down on that. But if my milk was good enough for Lorenzo, it was good enough for me. It'd be like taking a vitamin with all those "breast is best" nutrients, right? During the Depression, didn't whole starving villages survive on the milk from one woman's boobies?

I defrosted a bottle from our freezer stash. It was about a month old. We could have just licked it like a momsicle, but Jenni didn't want a brain freeze. After microwaving it, I poured the milk into four shot glasses. We held them up to drink.

Roger, show off, downed his right away. He said, "It's clumpy like mashed potatoes." I should have nuked it a little longer.

Jenni shot hers like the pro she is. She said, "Like soy milk with a Splenda."

I drank mine. It was the first shot I'd had in ten months, and it tasted like shit! Generally, I only like milk if it's diluted with Kahlua. That would have made a world of improvement.

Jionni shot his last. He was pretty cool about it, but I could tell he wasn't going to break into our stockpile of bottles for his morning cereal.

Medela and I grew really close. My pump was my best friend. We went shopping, to the salon, out to dinner. She came along on my first girls' night out after giving birth. Jenni, Ryder, and a couple other guidettes went out for a few cocktails and hit the club, just like the old days. Only this time, I would have to drain my boobs in the limo on the way there.

One of the girls asked, "You're bringing a backpack to the club?" Was I a mother, or a drug dealer?

"It's my pump," I said. "I thought I'd do a little on the way there so my boobs aren't sore, and don't leak all over the place when I'm dancing. Jenni, you should try it."

I really wanted her to feel the suction. I wanted *all of them* to experience the Super Suck. We were pretty drunk already. Jenni was willing to let my pump go to second base with her. Slut!

Ryder said, "It might deflate her implant!" We howled at that. It would have been pretty hilarious to see the bottle fill up with saline solution.

Jenni pulled down her bra, and held the flange up to her boobies. I flipped the switch. The pump kicked in, and Jenni's eyes bugged *out*. She pulled the thing off like it was trying suck out her soul! Now she had a taste of what I'd been going through.

I danced like a banshee that night. I didn't pump enough beforehand. My boobs ran like a river and the entire front of my dress was soaked. I was too drunk to notice or care. The whole next day, I had to pump and dump. I could smell the sake bombs in the bottle. My milk was so full of alcohol, I could have used it to start a bonfire in the yard. I could have cleaned the toilet with it. We broke out the alcohol test strips. I dipped one into the milk like a chemist in a lab. The strip nearly melted. Seeing the proof that what I put into my body was exactly what would come out of it changed my attitude about drinking even more than my skull-cracking hangover and the guilty feeling that I'd let myself down. I'd let Lorenzo down, too. He lost a day's worth of milk for that one night of partying. That wasn't fair to him.

I've barely had a sip of alcohol since that night.

My pump and I broke up after about three months. I had to do some traveling and wasn't able to pump every three hours. In only a few days of not keeping a rigid suck schedule, my breasts dried up. My boobs killed like they were engorged, but nothing came out. It was both a relief to stop pumping and a disappointment. I wanted to do it for a full year. Next time, I'll take all the vitamins, stay on schedule, and make sure the dairy farm doesn't close until I'm ready.

Three months of engorgement, de-gorgement, and stretched

nipples left me with ruined boobs. They're like floppy, deflated beach balls. My plan is to have three more babies, and then I'll get implants put inside the hanging skin. The milk service will be closed, but I'll be raring to go!

Chapter 18

Shit Happens

———∞———

Just as I predicted, Lorenzo was a genius of poop. He got that trait from me. I'm so proud of the little squirt.

The first day we brought him home, he shat on my leg, the couch, his bed, and the floor. It wasn't because he was rolling around bare-assed. We kept him in diapers with a thick layer of butt paste, believe me. There was just so much of it, it oozed out of his crap catcher.

I'd fretted about whether I'd gag while changing him, like that time I had to run from the room when I tried to change my nephew's diaper. I'm happy to report the good news: I adored my baby's shit! As I hoped, wiping and changing wasn't gross with my own kid. Not that it smelled like roses, but it wasn't bad at all. Just healthy human business. Even his farts smelled wholesome. He'd toot, and I'd say, "You're so cool." I loved it. Is that weird? I got misty-eyed doing anything I could for him, including wiping his ass. What a relief, not to feel sick doing the most basic mommy job. For a while, it seemed like all I did was pump and change Lorenzo's poopie pants.

The shit show was truly spectacular. I *oohed* and *ahhed* like I was at fireworks on the Fourth of July. It was just as colorful inside his diapers. I couldn't believe what came out of a baby's ass. At first, it was black tar, like alien scat. Then it was green. Then yellow. Breast milk poop looked like mustard juice with brown seeds, and smelled like a dish of cream cheese left on the counter for a few days. It was horrible, but healthy. I came to associate the smell with relief. It meant he was eating well. "Diaper Gold" we called it. We'd open up his diaper and declare, "Struck gold again!" Before long, we were mining for chocolate nuggets.

He always gave us a hint, his pre-verbal warning that a real gusher was on the way. Lorenzo would frown and grunt cutely. He'd make a photogenic duck face and . . . sploosh! We were swimming up Shit River.

Honestly, the sheer quantity cracked us up. How could a tiny body produce so much? It would overflow his diaper, seep up his back, and migrate all the way up into his hair. Jionni and I had to get a pair of scissors and trim the shit out of Lorenzo's hair. Sounds gross, but it was hilarious, a great experience to have with your husband-to-be. We laughed about his shitty haircut for hours. On no sleep, just about anything can make you giddy. But that one was a winner. We also fell down laughing when Lorenzo pooped in his bathwater. He loved doing that. He laughed and grabbed at the little floaters. I have to confess, that did look like a lot of fun. I might want to give it a try myself.

Our baby christened nearly every square foot of our house with his turds. A few times, we got to witness the phenomenon of "explosive diarrhea." The phrase pretty much sums up the actual experience, which has to be seen to be believed. I was in the middle of changing him, and he let loose. I was splattered, like a chocolate shake shot out of a cannon. I never loved my son more than when he painted the walls that day. It wasn't fun to clean up, that was for sure. But in all my life, I'd never been so amazed by the bodily functions of another human being. Lorenzo took me to another level of appreciation for our species.

I could probably clean up anyone's shit at this point. Having a baby teaches you that shit happens! *A lot* of shit happens. It's just a biological function. Poop, pee, puke, drool, snot. Babies and adults are leaky, juicy, wet sacs of one fluid or another. We leak some sort of moist gunk from every one of our holes, be it boogers, earwax, tears, or crap. That's the way we are from the day we're born until the day we dry up and die.

If you really think about it, a dirty diaper contains the whole human cycle of life, wrapped up into one stinkin' little package.

Some deep shit right there. And I do mean that literally.

Chapter 19

Lorenzo Has Two Moms

───∽◦∮◦∾───

From day one, Jionni was the most amazing mother I'd ever seen. He changed diapers, got up in the middle of the night, and gave Lorenzo his baths. He did everything for the baby that a mother could do (except pump—clearly that was my job). Jionni had to go to work during the day. But when he came home, the first words out of his mouth were, "Where's my baby?" He was so excited to see Lorenzo that sometimes he forget to kiss hello.

Yup, Lorenzo had two mommies. It was like Jionni and I were the same sex, because we hardly ever had sex.

There was never any question that we'd be full-time, equal parents, sharing all the joys and jobs fifty-fifty. Granted, we got a lot of help from our families. Living at Jionni's parents' was excellent for us, the baby, and his proud grandparents. Thanks to their pitching in during the first month, Jionni and I could grab naps or go out for an hour to the salon or a restaurant. When I had to travel for work or go to the city for a meeting, I arranged my schedule around Jionni's. We could usually work it out so one of us was home with Lorenzo. If we couldn't manage that, we'd ask our parents. They loved to babysit.

Friends had warned me that I might get frustrated with Jionni. A lot of dads didn't pull their weight when caring for an infant. But as I said, Lorenzo didn't have a dad. He had two moms, and we both wanted to do it all for the baby. Jionni and I argued about who got to change and feed Lorenzo. My fiancé couldn't wait to roll up his sleeves and dive in. He would wake up three times a night to bring the baby a bottle. We actually fought over who got out of bed at 4:00 AM to clean shit off the sheets. As soon as we heard that squeaky cry, we'd elbow each other out of the way to get to the crib first.

That only lasted for a few weeks. Then both of Lorenzo's tired mothers foisted middle-of-the-night feedings off on each other. It made no sense, really. A turf war over who got to inhale shit fumes? These days, we're like, "You get him. It's your turn."

At first, though, Jionni was such a devoted, single-minded mom, I got jealous of my own baby. My fiancé ignored me and gave all his attention to Lorenzo. He cuddled and kissed the baby all night, and barely touched me. We used to be as affectionate and all over each other as puppies in a basket. But then all of Jionni's hugs were given to our son. Which was great! Except that it totally sucked. I had to beg my man for kisses. Even with my porn star boobs, we really lost the spark for a while there. I guess he didn't think my nursing bras were sexy.

Like many new moms, Jionni was very particular. He had to make sure the baby care was done the right way. We bickered about it. He corrected me about technique, how to hold the bottle, how to burp, what speed to set the swing, when to put Lorenzo down for a nap. We were equally clueless in the hospital with our baby skills. And then, on the drive home, Jionni turned into some kind of expert.

When I went to pick up the baby, he would say, "Let me show you how it's done." I started to suspect it wasn't only criticism. Correcting me was Jionni's sneaky way of taking Lorenzo out of my arms so he could hold him. We both craved the closeness, and as equal mommies, we felt like we each had the magic touch. We fought a lot. I got really upset. Good mommies knew how to share.

Jionni criticized me (or, as he said, "joked") about whether I went to Lorenzo's crib fast enough when he cried. He once said, "I'd better give Lorenzo a bath so he doesn't smell like Mommy."

Funny. I nearly cracked his skull laughing.

Yeah, I took it personally! Jionni was a mommy, yes. Fine. But he wasn't the one who went through nine months of pregnancy. He wasn't pumping his nipples off every three hours. When he "joked" with me, it hurt my hormonally-fueled feelings. When he kept pestering me to wipe Lorenzo with a downward motion, I saw red (also brown).

I guess, in this way, Jionni's maternal instant was a let down. He could mommy Lorenzo, but I wanted him to be the daddy, too. I wanted him to know that I needed to be cuddled and kissed and told "I love you" and "You're doing great!" as much as our baby. A daddy would say, "You're the mother of my child and I worship you."

Here's Jionni

I did tell Nicole those things! She just wasn't satisfied unless I told her a dozen times a day. The bickering in the beginning about how I didn't cuddle enough was from both of us being so tired. And the criticism was just joking around. I was giving her shit, like we always used to do. The pregnancy was over, and I thought we'd just move back into laying into each other a bit more. I noticed that I was getting under her skin. But I was never serious about it! I blamed the lingering hormones on her reaction. It didn't last. We got back to normal. I don't remember how. But we did.

A few weeks after giving birth, I locked myself in my closet for a half an hour and emerged wearing the first decent outfit I'd put on in six months. I felt sexy and good about myself, despite our bickering and arguing about parenting.

Jionni said, "Look at you. You just had a baby?"

That was it. With just those two sentences from my man, I felt good about us again, and the spark came roaring back. I felt *seen*. Jionni looked at me, and he saw *me*. For a while there, he had Baby Tunnel Vision, and could only see Lorenzo. I was just an extension of the baby in Jionni's eyes. And then he noticed me again and remembered I was my own person. He would say he was just paying me a compliment. But it ran deeper than that to me.

When you become a mother, you still have desires and needs of your own. After giving birth, you want to be babied a little yourself. Not getting that from Jionni bugged the shit out of me. But you know what? He was just as exhausted as I was. He gave all of his energy to Lorenzo, like any good mom would.

Mom, dad, whatever. I don't really care about gender roles. What matters is doing what comes naturally and not worrying about who does what, or whether one of you is doing it more right than the other person. Your baby won't care if you wipe downward or sideways. He only cares if you use enough butt paste. As long as both parents are doing their share of the job, you'll have a happy family. Jionni and I are both Moms. We're both Dads. And we're all right with that.

This one website called me a "feminist mom." I read that and thought, *Someone understands me!* I define feminism as being honest about yourself. It's not trying to be a certain way, or playing a particular role, or enforcing a list of rules. Jionni is a feminist mom, too. We're just like every other parent of either gender who's doing his or her best and trying to have a good time while we're at it. Feminist moms don't sugarcoat the reality of being a parent. The truth is, motherhood is a bitch—and a bastard!—and it's awesome.

Chapter 20

Back to Myself

At the end of my pregnancy, all I wanted to do was give birth and then get back to normal. I missed all of the things I couldn't do, like dye my hair and go tanning—and get wasted.

About a month after Lorenzo was born, I went on a Girl's Night Out with Jenni, Deena, Ryder, and our friends Laura and Nina. We had a few vodka shots before we left the house. In the limo to the club, we popped open a bottle of Champagne, and had more vodka. Up until that night, I had consumed only one glass of wine all year. So I was drunk before we hit the highway. All those windows in the big backseat can make even the most seasoned limo rider feel queasy. My poor friend Nina was facing sideways—the absolute worst—especially doing 65mph on the Garden State Parkway with a glass of Champagne in one hand and a shot of vodka in the other. It was too much for her. She puked all over Ryder before we even got to the club. Ryder wasn't very sympathetic. I can't say I blamed her. I wouldn't want to dance smelling like half-digested tuna, either. The driver took Nina home and went to a car wash while we were partying inside. You better believe he got a *huge* tip that night!

When your friend vomits before you even get to the club, it's a bad omen. But we had a blast that night. After Champagne we switched to sake bombs—a shot glass full of sake dropped into a beer. Four different kinds of alcohol were pushed through my pregnancy-scrubbed liver. I got *twisted*. After being a saint for ten months, I had no idea what my tolerance level was anymore. I blacked out, and only found out what happened the next day.

Jenni called in the morning and filled me in. Apparently, I managed to pack a lot of trouble into just a few hours, including giving all the girls a lap dance, making out with, er, everyone, practically assaulting Laura by shoving my leaking boobs in her face, and dancing hard enough to make my sewn-up vagina fall out (it didn't, thank God). In my defense, I wasn't the only one who got raucous. As Jenni said, it was like a guidette sorority house. But I was definitely the instigator. I had a lot of time to make up for. I went hard that night. I didn't feel it was my choice. Crazy just happened to me, like an alien abduction.

On the way home, I screamed out the limo window, "I'm a mom!"

Even when I was blackout drunk, I was thinking about Lorenzo.

But that wasn't going to help me the next day when I had a lethal hangover and couldn't get out of bed. Jionni kept poking me to get up. When I could finally lift my head, I pumped my boobs (so glad I didn't leave Medela behind in the limo!). The milk was like rocket fuel and had to be dumped.

Jionni asked, "What went on last night?"

I knew it had been filmed and that Jionni would find out the truth. I had to tell him what happened, but I didn't have the mental focus or strong stomach to say it to his face. I pulled a passive-aggressive move and texted him. "I blacked out last night, and made out with Jenni," I wrote. I also told him that I was sorry and wouldn't do it again. Obviously, I knew he wouldn't be happy to hear the news. Remember, this is the guy who flew seven hours to visit me in Italy, and left two hours later when he got angry with me for losing control. He expected me to respect him by not degrading myself. But I was just acting up. That was who I was. I enjoyed having a few drinks and a good time.

To him, my text was a blow to his pride. He read it while sitting right next to me on the couch. He scooped up Lorenzo and said, "Stay away from me."

It was an ice pick to my heart. Seeing his back as he took my son up the stairs chilled me to the core. If I didn't know shame before that moment, well, I was starting to get the idea. I sat alone for a while, crying in agony with my hangover headache throbbing in my ears. My phone pinged.

A text from my fiancé. "You're a coward and a horrible mother and fiancée," he wrote.

Did it get any worse than that? The combo of physical pain, guilt, shame, and then being taken to task by the most important person in my life? Awful. Jionni is a very intense, sensitive person. I wasn't sure he was going to forgive me that time.

Was it really so terrible to make out with four girls in public, blacked out on sake bombs while my fiancé and newborn waited at home?

I didn't think so at the time. But now, seeing it from Jionni's perspective . . . I wasn't so sure. If Jionni got wasted at a club and made out with four of his friends, I'd be okay with it. But he wasn't me. He had his own ideas and opinions. In a relationship, you have to take the other person's feelings into account. You know what they call someone who doesn't do that? Single.

Along with being the love of my life, Jionni was the father of my son. I had to make this right.

He came back downstairs to the basement. I apologized to him, and told him he hurt my feelings, too. Even if he was angry—I'd never seen him *this* angry—he shouldn't text such cruel things to me.

He asked, "Is there anything else you need to tell me about last night?"

"I also made out with Ryder and Deena. And maybe Laura, too," I confessed. "But that's it!"

It was like tearing a scab off. His eyes turned cold, like he didn't even know me. "Pack your bags and get out," he said.

Hysterical, I took a drive around the block and called Jenni. She was on my side, of course, because she's my Boo. She also knew what I was capable of when blacked out. In a certain light, I was on good behavior that night, compared to other nights before I met Jionni or got pregnant.

"He told me I wasn't the mom or the fiancée he wanted," I told her. Jionni had also mentioned something about rehab.

Jenni said, "Jionni chose to be with you, he chose to get you pregnant, he chose to propose to you. He has to choose to be with the real you. You don't need rehab. You just needed a break."

Thank God for Jenni. She was my sounding board, and let me get it all out. But our conversation did make me question who the "real me" was. I wasn't a 21-year-old kid anymore. I was a 25-year-old mother. I couldn't just say, "My way or the Parkway. Accept me or forget me." Jionni and I had a baby! The thought of breaking up, fighting over custody, and being apart was terrifying. Any fight is ten times worse when children are involved.

His point was that a good mother and loving fiancée wouldn't behave like a sex addict mental patient on furlough. My point was that it was just one night of going overboard after ten months of being a saint. I had no intention of getting bombed every night, or even *any* night in the future. I saw it as a one-time letting loose kind of thing. He had to forgive me.

The old "real me," pre-baby, would have crawled back into bed and sulked for a few days. I would have only thought about my own hurt feelings. But I'd changed. This fight wasn't really about me being true to myself, or a woman's right to make a drunken fool of herself. It was about compromising for the sake of our family. I took out my pink leopard print notebook and wrote down a few points to bring up later, if I could get Jionni to talk to me. I needed to write my thoughts down so I would remember the words later on.

I went out and got a feast for us. Jionni's heart would definitely soften over sushi. (Sushi fixes everything.) I went to our favorite place and got a ton of takeout. I brought it home and set it out for us. That got him to the table.

He'd calmed down by then, and actually smiled at me. He wanted to work things out, too.

"What's in the book?" he asked.

I put it right next to the sushi. He couldn't not notice it. "I wrote some things down," I said, and read my notes. "When you get angry, you say really mean things. I don't want you do that anymore. It hurts my feelings. If we have fights, it's between me and you, and not Lorenzo. Love me even when I mess up. You have to still love me and not hate me."

"I always love you," he said. "I was discussing last night only."

"Don't bring up the past," I read. That was a big thing for us.

"I'm going to work on that. You can't go by what I said. It's not true. I do love you for who you are. I was wrong for saying those things. I was pissed."

He regretted his words. I regretted my actions. Well, okay, then! We apologized and made up. We both wanted this family to work. I vowed then and there that I'd stop drinking. I didn't ever want to fight like that with Jionni again. It was fucking scary. I hated it. I just can't make out with girls again. No major loss.

If I wasn't going to drink anymore—and I'd barely had a drop since my egg hatched—what *was* I going to do? I decided to start getting super healthy and back into shape.

During the pregnancy, my attitude was, "I'm fat. Deal with it."

But now that I'd been through the experience and was starting to feel like myself again, I wanted to get back in shape and be a fit mom for Lorenzo. I'd have to drop some pounds if I wanted to run errands with him on my hip. I didn't want to lose my breath putting his stroller in the car. Just rocking him to sleep required stamina. My arms felt sore after bouncing him. Nope, I had to start working out and building up my muscles to enjoy my new life to the fullest. The extra weight wasn't going to just disappear, though. I had to burn it off.

I was told that it wasn't safe to exercise until six weeks postpartum. I had to wait it out, and felt frustrated the whole time. I've heard the phrase, "Nine months on, the rest of your life to take it off." I thought it would be impossible to get rid of all the weight I gained—forty plus pounds—at least, impossible to get rid of fast. I might never get rid of all of it, which depressed me. My vision of motherhood was to be a hot mom, a MILF. I couldn't picture myself as a normal mother in baggy sweats and white sneakers driving a minivan.

As soon as I cleared the six-week hurdle, I called my old friend and trainer, Anthony Michael, and started hitting the gym. The first twenty pounds came off pretty quickly, thanks to working out and milking my boobs. Breastfeeding burned 500 calories a day! I pumped every three hours to get out every drop of the good stuff, and to burn every possible calorie. It was like doubling my workout, but all I had to do was lie on the couch and watch TV.

After dropping the first twenty, I hit a plateau. For the next two months, Anthony pushed me through a 90-minute daily workout, but my weight stayed about the same. I didn't realize I was replacing fat with muscle. But then the muscles emerged and my clothes got big. By the time Lorenzo was six months old, I managed to take off all the weight. Forty-four pounds. A lot of people have asked me how I did it. I used three revolutionary strategies. Prepare yourself for breaking news. This is totally outside the box:

I busted my ass.

I didn't give up.

I ate healthy.

No magic bullet. No pill. No secret powder. No laxatives, contrary to the trash some people write about me. I did it the old-fashioned way: I sweated my balls off!

My Workout

I committed to a daily 90-minute workout that included an hour of Plyometrics. Plyometrics is a muscle confusion method of explosive jumps and lifts. You're just standing there, and then—bam— you jump on top of a two-foot high box. Your muscles are like, *What the fuck is going on?* Blood rushes into them and makes them grow stronger and bigger in less time than if you just jogged or walked at an even speed. With Anthony, I do a combination of stuff on the mat and with weights.

Jumping jacks. Yeah, just like when I was a kid, except badass. Sometimes, the jumping jacks are just regular style, starting with your legs and arms open like a starfish, and then jumping the legs together, hands clapping over your head. But to confuse the muscles, I do a set with clapping, arms parallel to the floor and in front of me, Flipper style. After twenty reps, you will bark like a seal.

Box jumps. Stand facing a steel or metal platform, legs slightly apart. Bend at the knees and explode up and jump onto the box. Then jump off backward to where you were standing . . . and jump onto the box again, right away. Two sets of these, I pant for air. Five, nearly dead. My trainer has me do a set of ten.

Planks. Oh, man. They look so easy, right? Anthony has me do a plank—up on my palms and toes, arms straight, facing the floor, flat back. I need the upper body workout because I have little T. Rex arms. After holding the plank for a few seconds, I move my left hand to cover the right, putting all my strength on one arm. Then I move the left hand back and cover it with the right, shifting all my weight to the other side. Meanwhile, my back is screaming from holding the plank for so long. Your whole body shakes after ten reps.

Burpees. Sadistic! You start in standing position with your arms at your sides, and do a vertical jump as high as you can, arms pointing up to the ceiling. When you land, you drop your palms to the floor and kick the legs out into a plank. Immediately, you jump your feet back up to your hands. Then you lift your arms over your head—throw in a BURP to let out the air—and do another vertical jump. I'm sweating just writing about this move. You will seriously die after ten of these.

Lunge jumps. Start in a lunge position, one leg in front of the other. Both legs are in a deep knee bend, as deep as you can go. The back knee is almost on the floor. Arms are bent at the elbow at a ninety-degree angle, fists tight. Then—BAM—you explode out of the crouch into a vertical jump, fingers open, arms reaching for the ceiling, legs open. You land on the opposite side, and go immediately into a deep lunge knee bend with the opposite leg in back. Twenty of these and your thighs will burn.

Shuffle jumps. I feel like an Olympic speed skater when I do these. Start by standing on your right leg, left leg hovering a few inches off the floor. Then jump to the side, a big jump, landing on your left leg, with the right hovering over the floor. Balance on one leg, then shuffle jump back to the right leg. Meanwhile, your arms are swinging back and forth like you are building momentum on the ice. Do twenty laps around the rink, and your outer quads will pop.

Push-ups. Not a normal push-up! Normal push-ups are for pussies compared to Plyometric push-ups. Go down like a normal push-up as low as you can, boobs almost touching the mat. Then push up so quick and hard that your hands come up off the floor, like a hop. You land on flat palms, and go down again. At first, I couldn't do one of these. Now, I can do ten. Oh, yeah, I'm a baller.

Anthony and I also use weight machines to get the same effect, with sudden bursts of muscle power. You have to do everything with proper form or you might hurt your joints. It's a good idea, I feel, to do at least one or two sessions with a trainer to get the moves exactly right before you do the workout on your own.

To cool down after an hour of jumping and lunging and making my muscles beg for mercy, I do 30 minutes on the treadmill. I can now run two miles in 18 minutes, and then I walk for another mile to cool down. It's funny that I used to think walking on the treadmill was my whole workout! Well, that was before I went through a pregnancy and gained over forty pounds. My body changed, and I had to change my workout.

I love Anthony to death, but a girl can do only so many platform jumps before she wants to scream or throw the box out of the window. So when I get bored with trainer sessions, I take a spin class or do kickboxing or Zumba. In Zumba, you get to shake your ass and frolic to an African beat. Love it.

You *have* to love your workout, whatever it is. If you don't, it won't last. You can keep it going for a year on sheer willpower, *maybe*. But to really stick with it, you need willpower, a sense of fun, and motivation. Why do I kill myself at the gym for 90 minutes at least five days a week?

I do it for Lorenzo. He's the only motivation I need. He's starting to crawl now. Soon enough, he'll zoom around the house like a Ninja baby. His favorite pastime is for me to hold him under the armpits on my lap, and he does his little baby Plyometric moves, jumping on my thighs. He's going to be just as athletic as his dad. And I have to be fit and strong so I can keep up with both of them. Every squat and lunge and push-up I do now is insurance for the future that I'll have the strength and stamina to chase after Lorenzo—and his three brothers or sisters to come. It's going to take a lot of energy to run all over town, keeping up with four kids and their school, activities, and play dates. I'm going to need to be Super Mommy, with super buns and guns.

My Diet

My life used to be about looking good for the camera and feeling good in a sensual way (getting drunk, smutting, pigging out). Now I only want to feel strong in a mental and physical sense. Feeling good means building my muscles and putting only healthy food into my body.

For the first two-and- a-half months after giving birth, whatever I put into my body came out through my boobs and into my milk. I wanted it to be pure and taste good for Lorenzo. You know how you can go to Whole Foods and get milk from grass-fed-only California cows who get daily massages and whatnot? Well, I wanted to be like that healthy cow. I also wanted to make sure Lorenzo loved his milk. I ate whatever would make it taste creamy and rich for him. Ice cream, lots of cheese, and red meat. When my milk dried up, though, I cut way back on fat and carbs and upped the protein. My trainer Anthony's company has a food delivery service called Express Fitness Meals. For $30 a day, they deliver meals and snacks right to my door. I'm not a cook, at all. So having someone else take care of that for me keeps my calorie count—about 1,300 a day—in check. I don't have to shop for and prepare my food, and can spend more time with Lorenzo. A few sample menus for a typical day:

Breakfast

Egg white omelet. My friend Dr. Oz is a big fan of protein in the morning to give you energy throughout the day. I do what he says. If you cut out the yolks, eggs are as light as air. My omelets have five egg whites (only 75 calories), a half a cup of broccoli florets (15 calories), and are cooked with a half a teaspoon of healthy coconut oil (60 calories). Even someone as awkward in the kitchen as I am can make this. You whisk the whites until they're fluffy. Heat up the oil until it glazes the pan. Pour in the eggs. When it gets a little brown around the edges, pour the chopped broccoli on one side. Fold it over, and flip it a couple times for fun. That's it.

Fruit cup. I don't care if fruit has sugar and is packed with carbs. It tastes great and is full of vitamins. It's practically the only sweet food I eat, and I'm not giving it up! I love it all: pineapple, berries, citrus, grapes. I chop it up into pieces and eat a small bowl of fruit salad every morning. Even the sweetest cup of fruit isn't going to be more than 100 calories.

Total: Around 250 calories. I eat the same breakfast nearly every day. I keep it from getting boring by changing some of the ingredients. I mix up the kinds of fruit in the salad. I substitute spinach or peppers for broccoli. If I feel like I'm going to crazy if I have one more omelet, like I might throw the pan out the window, then I know it's time to have something completely different for a few days, like yogurt or oatmeal with fruit.

Lunch

I rely on Express Meals for lunch. It's just so easy to open the package and dig in, no worries about portion size, calories, or ingredients. Anthony's meals are dairy free. This is a huge plus for me because it means no gassssss! A few of my faves:

Turkey tacos. God, I love these! They're 99% lean turkey meat cooked in a little olive oil with low sodium taco seasoning in a whole wheat shell, with romaine lettuce, avocado, salsa, and light cheddar cheese on top. So good.

Chicken salad. Grilled chicken with cranberries and goat cheese on a big mound of greens, tossed with light balsamic vinaigrette. I love chicken for protein. The greens fill me up.

Wrap sandwich. Anthony has one called "The Italian," with grilled chicken, roasted red peppers, basil, and fresh low-fat mozzarella, stuffed with spinach and rolled in a whole wheat tortilla.

Flat bread pizza. The flat bread pizzas are the size of a personal pizza you'd get at a restaurant, with a no-sugar homemade tomato sauce and 2% mozzarella with basil and bits of either chicken or steak.

Total: Depends on the meal, but all of the choices are around 350 calories.

Dinner

More Express Meals, or just stuff I can cook for myself.

Burger! I love to have a burger because it's yummy, and you can order it in any restaurant. But skip the bun. That's where the carbs come in, and I don't want them or need them. To hold the carbs, I wrap the burger in lettuce leaves, and stuff pickle and tomato slices in there, too. Ketchup is basically red sugar, so I skip it. Instead, I use Dijon mustard. I also order a side salad with vinaigrette.

Meat and Two Veg. My classic dinner is usually some grilled chicken or fish with all kinds of seasoning and healthy marinades, like lemon dill or low-sodium teriyaki, with a steamed green vegetable like asparagus or broccoli and a baked sweet potato. Love, love, love steamed cauliflower. I make a full plate, and I never feel hungry afterward. The main thing is portion control. Some men can order a

16-ounce steak and suck that thing right down. I try to keep my steak in the six-ounce range. Otherwise, it's more food than I need, but I'd eat it all if it was in front of me.

Total: Around 500 calories.

Dessert

I give myself permission to eat something sweet but small every day. Another fruit bowl. Protein chocolate chip cookies. Almond fudge brownies are the absolute best. I used to think that almond butter could never satisfy like real butter. Or that agave was no substitute for sugar. But I was wrong. When I eat using healthy ingredients, my taste changes to like them better than the other stuff. If I tried to eat regular butter, sugar, or flour now, I'd feel kind of sick.

Total: Depending on the dessert, around 100 calories.

Snacks

I keep my metabolism going by splitting my meals into smaller portions. That way, I never get hungry during the day. The one time I do get that empty feeling is right before bed—the worst time to eat. If I eat too much, I get nightmares about screaming goats with evil eyes (seriously). But if I don't eat at all, well, I get hungry! I don't ever want to feel deprived because that's when binges happen. So I make a snack, such as:

Brown rice cakes with almond butter. The almond butter is low in carbs, high in protein, and totally hits the spot. Two of these, and I don't need another bite.

Yogurt and fruit. A graham cracker crust cup (you can buy them at any supermarket) with half a cup of low-fat yogurt, two dollops of Cool Whip, and fresh fruit on top. Yum.

Total: Only 150.

Grand total for the day: Around 1,500.

Some days I eat more, some days less. It's just a ballpark number that works for me. It seems like hardly any calories, but I eat continually all day long, including a dessert and snacks. I'm a pretty small person, so I don't need as many calories as someone larger than me. One day a week, I splurge and have ice cream and chips. I make up for it by adding time to my workout the next day. Watching what I eat has helped me get back down to my pre-pregnancy weight of 105 pounds. This is the weight where I feel healthiest, and it's where I want to stay . . . until the next pregnancy.

When I visited my mom's secret boyfriend Dr. Oz on his show recently, he asked if I ever worried that dieting would trigger a recurrence of the anorexia I had back in high school. Matt Lauer asked me if I had an unhealthy body image to work that hard to lose weight so quickly after giving birth. Gossip magazines wrote that the only food I ate was egg whites, and that all my friends were terrified I was starving myself to death.

Completely wrong. Not even close. Does an anorexic eat ice cream? Does she have popping arm muscles? An anorexic wouldn't have the strength to battle back the bullshit. I look at the gossip rags and laugh. It's hysterical how people make up stories to sell magazines. They should see me eat my pizza! It's ludicrous and annoying, though, to see my picture with the words "Eating disorder" over my head. I'd never put my health at risk. I have a son to take care of.

In all fairness, 42 pounds is a huge amount of weight to drop in six months. I do still complain that I hate the remnants of my mommy pouch and that my boobs look like deflated balloons. But I'll never have an eating disorder again. I was immature. I starved myself because I was desperate to keep my place as a flyer on the cheerleading team. I didn't need a full-on intervention. When the school nurse brought it up, I agreed with her. I said to myself, "You're hurting yourself. This is stupid. Stop it," and that was it. I started eating again. Purposefully weakening myself would defeat the purpose of what I'm trying to do, which is get in great physical condition. My goal isn't to be skinny. It's to be strong and full of energy for Lorenzo. I'm eating super healthy and exercising for that purpose, and it's working! I can lift Lorenzo and hold him while he bounces on my lap for a hour—great for the biceps! I rock him in my arms to sleep—killer on the triceps! I carry him up and down the stairs—quads!

I got what I wanted. I'm a MILF and a Super Mom. Honestly, it just wasn't that hard. I thought it would be nearly impossible to get in shape and care for my kid. But it's totally doable. I just signed up for the food delivery and got myself to the gym. Once I'm there, I have a routine to follow, and 90 minutes goes by quickly. For sure, the hardest part is getting there. Having a trainer keeps me from getting lazy and prevents boredom. I go with my sister-in-law-to-be, who also just had a baby. I know it's harder for older moms. They just don't snap back as quickly. But I feel anyone can do it with the right motivation and determination.

It's all about Lorenzo. As long as he needs me, I need to work out. They go together. One day, maybe he'll come to the gym with me. Mommy & Me Plyometrics! Love it.

Chapter 21

Back in the Saddle

———∘∩∘———

There is one part of my body that isn't snapping back to its pre-pregnancy condition. My vagina will never be the same! Right after giving birth, it felt *used*, like I'd had sex for weeks without lube. It was stretched to the width of a Frisbee. Now, it's back to normal size. It looks more or less the same, not that I'm bending over a hand mirror and staring at it every day. But sex feels different now.

Thanks to postpartum hormones, I was horny for the first two weeks after giving birth, and couldn't wait for the six-week no-go period to end. When we could finally have sex again, though, the hormones faded and I lost my mojo. Jionni tried to sex me up. I was just so tired and wrung out. I'd been feeding and changing and caring for Lorenzo day and night. And now, I had to have sex? *Meh.*

We eventually did it when Lorenzo was three months old. I'm sorry to report that sex has changed, and not for the better. It hurts. I think it's because in the delivery room, when they were sewing me back together, I asked for an extra stitch. I might have gone one stitch over the line. Now it feel like my vagina has been sewn shut. The door is nearly closed. Just a tiny bit open. Jionni isn't the tallest guy around, but he's got a hefty braciola. He says sex feels the same for him. He doesn't feel that extra stitch like I do. I thought at least one of us would enjoy the tightness. Oh, well.

It's my dream to have three more kids, but at the rate we're going, we might never have sex again.

I exaggerate. Sort of. Along with my like-a-virgin vag and exhaustion, I had another problem. No sex drive. I just stopped wanting it. Sex used to be the number one motivator in my life. The possibility of getting lucky was what would get me out of bed at the crack of noon. I'd spend hours getting dolled, putting on a gaudy dress, gluing on my lashes, and teetering in high heels off to a club to find a man. Smutting was my favorite hobby. Flirting was my religion. Smushing was my *calling*. I thought about sex constantly, and wanted to do it all the time. I was so damn good at it, too. I took a lot of pride in my sexuality. I assumed it would never cool off.

Right now, my sexual spark couldn't ignite a backyard grill! Jionni and I are down to, like, once a week. I'd be lying if I said that we're off pace all because of me. Ha! If Jionni were begging for it, I'd lie there and take one for the team. But he's too tired for sex, too. In his pre-baby life, he wanted to do it every day. We're okay with a scaled-back erotic life. For both of us, the baby stole our sex drives. But what we got back was so much sweeter. I've heard that when the baby gets older, you get it back. But we're going to be having babies for a while. So I figure by 2020, we'll be raring to go.

Chapter 22

That's How We Roll (With a Stroller)

Our first family vacation was to Hollywood, Florida, to Jionni's family's vacation house. It was in the winter when Lorenzo was about four months old. We were so paranoid about taking him to the airport in the cold, we wrapped him up like a bubble boy. Hat, scarf, sweater, coat, fleece hoodie with footsies over that, under two blankets, and a cover on the stroller. He probably lost three pounds of sweat just getting from the house to the plane.

Me, too! We lugged along his car seat/stroller, which had to be dismantled at the gate, and a diaper bag bursting with milk bottles, diapers, wipes, and creams. Of course, I had a massive suitcase for myself, as well as suitcases for Lorenzo and Jionni. We brought along the baby bouncy seat, too, because Enzo loved it—and so did we. For three people to take one flight, we had enough luggage for an army.

"We can buy stuff there," Jionni said.

"In Florida?" I asked. "At the old people development?"

The house was in a retirement community. Just the old people and us. Lorenzo was the only baby for ten square miles. Jionni and I were the next youngest people by 40 years.

Whenever we left the condo, Lorenzo was in his vacation baby outfits of shorts and t-shirts. We drenched him in sun block. He can tan when he's eighteen. (Listen to me! I'm such a freaking *mother*!) I got the idea of my baby sunglasses line on this vacation. I kept propping my own shades on Lorenzo's tiny nose. *Babies need their own cool shades,* I thought. *Make a mental note.*

Jionni and I took walks around the development. We'd put Lorenzo in the stroller and tour the place. People looked at us, but only because we were strangers and, you know, not ancient. But no one recognized us. We went to the development pool a lot. Around it were a hundred oldies in lounge chairs, and the three of us. Lorenzo loved his swimmies and riding on a float. We hung at the pool with the ninety-year-olds and just splashed around all day. Going to the community club for dinner was like swimming through a sea of human fossils. At the beach, we were the only people for long stretches without wrinkles. *Must get an anti-wrinkle moisturizer in my line,* I thought. *Make another note.*

Going on vacation was very inspiring for my business.

It was over too quickly. The good times had to stop strolling. We packed up our little village and went back to the airport. That's about the time Jionni and I realized with a bit of a shock that we'd gone on vacation and *hadn't had one drink*. And it was, like, the best vacation ever. We were a family on our little family vacation. We got some sun, some fun, decent food, and alone time as a threesome.

No sex either. It wasn't about smushing in Florida. It was about cuddling, just me and my fiancé and baby. Lately, cuddling has made me feel even closer to my man than sex. It's a sad/happy truth about love. My feelings for Jionni are so deep, we don't need to go balls deep. When we do it, sex is fine (hoping it gets better than fine before too long!). But it's just not as important for us as it used to be to seal our relationship. We've got Lorenzo—he seals the deal.

Lorenzo was a good boy on the flight down, and slept the whole time. But on the way back to New Jersey, the baby was fussy. I had to walk up and down the aisle to calm him down. We were recognized again. Everyone on the plane took pictures. I was in mommy mode. I said, "Back off! You're too close to my baby!" I didn't care what they thought of me. If anyone tried to touch Lorenzo, I'd hiss and show my claws. And you know what? It was kind of fun to be a huge bitch. The whole trip was a lot of fun. I can see us taking family vacations every year. As we have more kids, we might need a separate plane for just the luggage.

Chapter 23

Next!

Having a baby forces you to live in the moment. Sometimes I'm so present, an entire day goes by in a blur. It's the Baby Time Warp. You wake up and start the routine of feeding, playing, diaper changing. Before you know it, it's time for sleep. A whole month goes by like that. Then nine months. I can't believe Lorenzo is standing up and starting to take baby steps. He's growing out of his clothes faster than we can do his laundry. I change his outfits a few times a day to make sure he wears it all at least once. He's a rock star in whatever he's got on. The kid's got swag. Just saying.

Lorenzo is stronger and faster every day. He's old enough for big boy pajamas. Soon, he'll tear around the house. Soon after that, he'll be going to school and having his own life. When I think about the future, I only think about it in terms of Lorenzo's milestones. His future and mine are melded together. I simply can't imagine my life without my baby by my side.

Baby Bumps

We are building a house on a lot near Jionni's parents in North Jersey. It's got six bedrooms, and I want to fill them up with tan babies. Four total. That'll leave one bedroom for guests. That room will *not* be taken up by a nanny. No judgment about anyone else using a nanny. But I don't like the idea of hiring a non-family member or friend to care for my kids. I don't trust just anyone. I only leave Lorenzo with people I know. Fortunately, between my parents and Jionni's huge family, we can always get a babysitter if we need one.

My friends are happy to babysit, too. Before I had Lorenzo, most of them thought they weren't anywhere ready to have kids themselves. Now they're obsessed with my baby and want their own. Before long, Lorenzo is going to be a wise older brother, cousin, and "cousin" to all my friends' kids.

I tell them, "Don't rush it. Enjoy not having kids for a while. Have fun with mine and start your family when you really feel the urge." When you have a baby, even going to the mall and getting your nails done is a major process. If someone isn't home to watch him, you have to load up the diaper bag, and lug him in the car seat. Then transfer him to the stroller, and hike up stairs or up the escalator. He might puke or shit himself, and then you have to change him. Or you can't maneuver the stroller into the ladies room and you (almost) pee or shit yourself.

You have to fend off old ladies who feel like they have the right to pinch the baby's cheeks or adjust his little hat. But I do sympathize with the impulse to reach out and touch a stranger's baby. I kind of want to hold every baby I see lately. I use to run away from them. Now I spot a baby at a restaurant, and my nipples burn from missing Lorenzo.

Don't get me wrong. I can't wait for my friends to have kids. I'll definitely be psyched when they have newborns, and I've got a five-year-old who can get his own juice and snacks.

So, yeah, my house! I can't wait for it to be finished. Even though it's been fantastic to live with Jionni's family, I'm done with cave dwelling. We need more space than the Man Cave (or is it the Baby Cave?). All of my clothes and shoes and Lorenzo's stuff are crammed into the corners. This is no way to raise a family. We need a place of our own. I don't want to get married—or start pregnancy number two—until we're moved in and settled. I hope it's ready by Lorenzo's first birthday. We'll throw him a huge party there.

Here's Jionni

We talk about the future a lot. The house, the next baby, getting married. My sister—the one who was pregnant when

Baby Bumps

Nicole was—is pregnant again. She's due in a few months. I have a big, close family and love that Lorenzo and our next kids will have cousins the same age. But we can't get pregnant again until we have a place to live. First we move, then we can get married. Then we'll have another baby.

But then again, accidents do happen.

Moving is going to be a big change, obviously. We won't have Jionni's mom cooking for us. I can barely boil water for pasta. I'm going to have to learn how to cook, do laundry, and clean house. That's cool. I want to live clean. No more clothes thrown all over, food on the counter, and clogged toilets for me. After living with a lot of roomies and family for so long, it'll be strange to have a place of our own. Our crew will visit, obviously. But it won't be like Grand Central with foot traffic all day like where we are now. I'll miss everyone, but it's a necessary step. I'm not a kid. I *have* a kid. I'm an adult, a mother, and a soon-to-be wife. I should have my own home with a yard for Lorenzo and his sisters and brothers. It might feel isolated at first, but we'll fill it up with kids. Who knows, in a few years, we'll probably outgrow it.

I'll complain that we need an even bigger house. I hope we do. I want to burst through the rafters with my family.

People ask if the old me is gone for good. Some of my former ways will not make a comeback. I don't even think about going drinking with friends. Booze would ruin my diet. It'd ruin my attitude. I want to keep my head on straight. It's a form of neglect, I feel, to spend all morning nursing a hangover instead of caring for your baby. If I do party my ass off again, it'll be on a weekend vacation with Jionni—if we ever take one! My parents or his will watch Lorenzo, we'll fly off somewhere for a couple of days, and then I'll do shots and stay up all night. Otherwise, nope.

I'm a grown up. That's the long and short of it. I used to be a little crazy. But I didn't kill anyone. I didn't do drugs. Partying at the Jersey Shore in the summers is just what people do if they grow up around here. If Lorenzo or my daughters do the same thing in twenty years, I'll probably be horrified, but I won't be surprised.

Apart from being fairly certain Lorenzo will watch us on YouTube one day (he'll be so embarrassed!), I have no idea what will happen in his life. But I do know that with my genes, he'll be short. Maybe he should be a jockey or a trapeze artist. My parenting goal is to just love him, let him live, and support him. I'll need to work a lot and expand my business to give him a good life, an easy life. I hate the idea of him struggling, ever. Of course, I want my children to understand the value of a dollar. They'll have jobs and chores. I just don't want them to stress out about their needs being met. I definitely don't aspire to raise him with a TV camera in his face. We signed on to do Season Three of *Snooki & JWOWW*. It will most likely be the last. I won't film away from my family, and I don't think it's healthy for Lorenzo to grow up on TV. When he's three or four and starts to clue in to the wider world, it's time to stop. Really.

Maybe I'll have other opportunities, and that'd be awesome. I can't plan for anything, though. We're being smart and saving money now. Jionni and I have already started a college fund for Lorenzo. Our only goal is to give him whatever he needs, and make sure he knows he'll always have a family to fall back on. That's what my parents did for me, and I want to return the favor for my kids.

The next big thing for me: Getting married! Jionni and I will do that right after we move into the house. And then, when we're legal, we'll try to get pregnant right away. And then again, and again. If we have our next three kids a year apart, I'll be done with all my pregnancies by age 30.

And *then*, finally, I'll get a boob job.

Epilogue

Mother's Day

My mom did it all for me. Now I know what she went through. Having a child has definitely brought us closer. Before, my parents were kind of annoying. Now, I can't wait to talk to them. They care about Lorenzo's poops as much as I do. Thank God someone does.

Growing up, I really got into Mother's Day. I would make a pilgrimage to the dollar store and pick out little gifts for Mom. I'd served her breakfast in bed, the whole deal. This Mother's Day, my first as a mom, was almost too exciting. I looked forward to it forever. I went back home to Marlborough and spent a four-day weekend with my mom and grandma. Jionni had to work. It was just Lorenzo and three generations of mommies. And it couldn't have been more special.

On Mother's Day morning, Mom put out a pair of hand-painted flowerpots on the table. She pointed at them and said, "Remember these?"

I did. When I was about ten—old enough to make something besides a crayon outline of my hand—I painted terra cotta flowerpots for her. Two of them. We planted a couple of geraniums in them and they looked beautiful.

"You still have them?" I asked.

"Some gifts you keep forever, no matter how old your kids get."

One day, Lorenzo will come home from school with a picture frame made of popsicle sticks, or a painted flower pot, and he'll give it to me with as much pride and excitement as I gave gifts to my mom. And I will treasure them and keep them forever.

She gave me a few gifts that weekend, too. She told me how proud she is of me. How wonderful it is for her to see me in mommy mode. She said she respects and appreciates the adult woman I've become. Thanks, Mom!

For his part, Lorenzo thought it was appropriate to drive me crazy. I felt it was because his father wasn't around. Lorenzo knows I will baby him, and he takes advantage of that. He decided not to sleep at all during the night, and play with mommy in bed from 2:00 AM to 4:00 AM for four nights straight. As I was sitting there with him, exhausted, I realized how lucky I am to have such an amazing, beautiful son. There's no doubt he can drive me nuts and stress me out at times. Doesn't matter. He's my son, my baby. I love him more than words can describe. I would do anything to make him the happiest boy in the entire world. Sometimes, you need to be so freakin' tired to see the truth. Keeping me awake at 2:00 AM to play with him, his smile and laugh, was his first Mother's Day gift to me. His whole existence was my Mother's Day present.

That's the gift I'll keep forever, no matter how old he gets. I love you, Lorenzo, for the next hundred Mother's Days and beyond.

XXOOXXOO,
Nicole

Acknowledgments

There are so many people to thank for the making of this book!

First of all, I'd like to thank Val Frankel for helping me make it readable (LOL). You're the best!

I'd like to thank my team Scott Talarico, Stacey Wechsler, Danny Mackey, Scott Miller, and my parents for always getting shit done and helping me achieve amazing goals!

Thank you, Jennifer Kasius and everyone at Running Press for publishing this book!! I know we are going to help a lot of mommies out there!

Can't forget my family! I'd like to thank my mom, dad, my in-laws Janis and Joe, and my sister-in-law Janelle for helping me through my whole pregnancy experience and dealing with my bullshit!

Also want to thank 495 Productions for making my last few months of pregnancy comfortable! You guys are the best!

Also want to shout out my bitches JWoww and Stephanie for being there for me and catering to all my pregnancy needs! I got your backs when yous are preggers!!

Last but certainly not least, I want to thank my AMAZING doc Dr. Russo and all the staff at St. Barnabas for helping me deliver my healthy baby boy! So sorry for the farts during labor. You're all amazing to me and I love you!!!